"MY LORD THEY ARE PRINTERS!"

R. W. FINCH
Organiser
SOGAT '82

LONDON CA&EP BRANCH, SOGAT '82

This edition published 1984 by
London CA&EP Branch, SOGAT '82

Printed in Great Britain by
Twentieth Century Press Limited
Bishop's Stortford, Herts

Quote from Defending Counsel:

My Lord they are Printers! They are dispensers of that glorious art which has rescued mankind from ignorance and slavery and conducted them to knowledge and to freedom! The art that has snatched man from the degraded posture and condition of a brute animal and placed him upon his feet, erect and looking upon Heaven!

Pressmen Apprenticeship Prosecution 1798

Contents

Acknowledgements

My sincere thanks are due to many who assisted in gathering the valuable information or gave access to those records without which it would have been impossible to write the stories outlined herein.

To Peter Gunter of Head Office Staff, who gave much of his own time in drawing many illustrations in reference to petitions of pardons and other illustrated letters and the valuable assistance on research I express grateful appreciation, also to the various secretaries who assisted in the copy.

In compiling the stories within this book I am conscious that many more ought to have been included, but research and time has been a determining factor, but it is clearly impossible to mention all who suffered and deserve mention.

Lastly, my grateful thanks go to Chris Robbins, Branch Secretary, and members of the London Branch of Clerical, Administrative & Executive Personnel whose financial and co-operative assistance allowed this book to be published.

Preface I

This is a book about the struggle of ordinary people. It is a book that tells the story of the development of SOGAT '82 over 200 years.

SOGAT '82 can rightly claim it is the oldest trade union in the world. In 1983 it celebrated its 200th anniversary as an industrial trade union, but its records go back to the 14th century.

I have often referred to the trade union movement as the only true society that I have known. Born out of conflict of yesteryear and matured in the savage, painful and bitter struggle following the industrial revolution, it still remains the only true society which represents the aims and aspirations of ordinary people.

All those hundreds of years ago workers recognised that there had to be a better way of life than long hours, starvation wages, bad conditions, where the majority of children were lucky to reach the age of maturity.

Well before the Tolpuddle Martyrs, members of this Union were being transported to Australia. A number were sentenced to death for daring to have the temerity to fight for a better way of life.

One cannot review the martyrdom of our forebears without drawing a parallel to what is happening in this country today, where we have a Government that has never hidden its deep hostility to the trade union movement – who have introduced laws which seek to attack what we have fought for and what our forebears have fought for over centuries – for what is under attack are the individual rights of ordinary working people and not just the trade unions.

In reading this book it has to be understood that under attack is the political freedom and the whole basis of democratic society, where opposition and dissent are the cornerstone of democracy.

I firmly believe, as indeed our forebears believed, that the only defence that working people have against repressive Governments is to combine within trade unions. Governments over the years have feared that the combining of workers would affect their pernicious policies, which react against the interests of the majority of the community.

We, the ordinary people of this country, have waited long and patiently for a socially just society. Yes, we have made considerable advances in the 200 years but as magnificent as our journey has been we still have a long way to go.

The real question this book poses is – are we to throw away all that we have worked for over a great number of years, and hand down to our children a society where people once again are in bondage?

Our forebears challenged the law as it stood in those days. Law is not an end to itself. To be true law it must nurture life and promote the common good. At this present moment laws are being introduced in this country that have no relationship to true law. I firmly believe that the society that we built with religious and political freedom came about because our forebears were prepared to challenge bad laws, which had the seeds of intolerance and injustice.

I firmly believe it is an essential requirement of any country which calls itself a democracy that there should be a free and independent trade union movement. This point of view is being challenged by this Government.

I personally have never seen the trade union movement other than one which challenges the excesses of a society which is politically and economically hostile to the needs of ordinary people.

Whilst in this book we are telling a story related to the past 200 years, I acknowledge that each generation has to fight its own battles. Each generation has to renew its commitments to win victories and sometimes taste the bitterness of defeat.

I say to those who read this book, let us salute those who went before us. They helped to lay the foundations. The greatest tribute we can pay to them is to re-commit ourselves on what they offered and suffered for. We owe it to them. We owe it to ourselves. We owe it to our children and indeed their children.

Bill Keys, *General Secretary*

Preface II

In the late 1910s clerical workers in the national newspaper offices of Fleet Street, London began to join the National Union of Clerks. Despite being recruited into a non 'printing union' the workers adopted the tradition of forming themselves into chapels.

By 1920 many chapels had been formed and came together as a Branch called the Newspaper, Printing & Publishing Clerks Guild (still part of the NUC).

One such Chapel was the 'People Chapel'. Its inaugural meeting was held on 13th January, 1920 at 6.00 p.m. and the members present endorsed the objectives of the Chapel which were:

a.   The safeguarding of the mutual interests in connection with their employment of the clerical staff of the People Ltd.

b.   To keep the clerical staff in close touch with the activities of the Branch.

c.   The furtherance of the interests of the Newspaper Printing & Publishing Clerks Guild in every possible manner.

d.   To be the medium for the collection of all data required for Trade movements in connection with the firm.

e.   To be the organising unit within the firm responsible for bringing into the Union all clerical workers.

f.   To promote friendly relations with other Trade Unions on the staff and to co-operate with the Chapels representing them.

g.   To see that the members of the Union on the staff pay their contributions and Union dues regularly.

h.   Such other objects as the Chapel with the approval of the Guild may from time to time determine.

For the members at the People the relationship with the NUC was shortlived, for on 3rd July, 1920 the minute book states:

> 'Chairman explains that owing to the fact that after July 3 members of this Chapel (NUC) will secede from the NUC and become part of the NSOPA it becomes necessary to dissolve the Chapel.'

The People Chapel in company with other Chapels in Fleet Street had now decided that their future lay with a print union.

During the month of July 1920 Allan Grant McLean, the Guild Secretary, led nearly 1,500 clerical workers into membership of the National Society of Operative Printers and Assistants.

Exactly 62 years later NATSOPA amalgamated with SOGAT '75 to form SOGAT '82, and so a group of white collar workers in the forefront of technological change in the 20th century forged a link in history with the Bookbinders of 1783.

There will no doubt, be new links forged in the future and new chapters of our history which will need to be written but it is important to remember the past struggles and individuals who were prepared to sacrifice themselves for the good of their brothers and sisters.

Bob Finch has with care and excellence pieced together some of the stories which make up the last 200 years of SOGAT.

This book is both a tribute to his work and to the memory of all 'our members' that you will meet as the pages unfold.

Christopher Robbins, Branch Secretary. *London CA&EP Branch*

Introduction

Very great difficulties lie in the path of research, as the earliest attempts at organisation of the Society date back over two hundred years, to a time when men were compelled to adopt a plan of secret association forbidden by the law and records of their early doings were either not kept or, those which may have been kept, were constantly handed from one person to another in secrecy for safe keeping until they had served their purpose. Then they were intentionally, or accidentally, destroyed.

Therefore, had it not been for the love of antiquarian research displayed by John Jaffray – Bookbinder, it is highly probable that any attempt today to unveil the mysteries of the early years of 1783–1788 would have been well nigh fruitless.

Of manuscripts very few remain, and even of the few printed notices of early proceedings which were made and published, some are not to be found even in the British Museum. For his early researches into 'The Journeymen Bookbinders Trade Society' John Jaffray seems not only to have ransacked all available documents at the time, but to have put himself to considerable trouble and expense in order to obtain information from the only surviving men (in 1846), whose memories might yield some missing link in the story of the early Trade Lodges of the Society.

It is without apology, therefore, that I have borrowed extensively from John Jaffray, and others of the early Trade Societies that have made SOGAT '82, for the earlier chapters of this book – because it would have been impossible to write without doing so – filling in other such details as I may have been fortunate enough to secure by further research.

It may appear to some that, having said 'without apology' I have a supreme contempt for the rights of others. But I say it with every feeling of gratitude to John Jaffray and others, and I believe John Jaffray in particular believed that he looked for someone to continue the work which he commenced. He in his day regretted that so many years had been allowed to pass away without an attempt being made to preserve an account of the deeds of the 'Friendlies' of a former time and, as he himself indicated, rescued from oblivion and for the first time put upon record that 'which time had almost swept from memory's page' expressing the hope, 'that the future historians of our trade may be enabled to detail every circumstance connected with these occurrences, the very smallest of which must prove interesting to all the Society's members.

Therefore, however unworthy, we take this matter up and, in order to make a complete story, shall borrow, without apology, from the work of our predecessors.

R. W. Finch
Organiser
SOGAT '82

1

The Men of the Combination

I will not cease from mental fight,
Nor shall my sword sleep in my hand,
Till we have built Jerusalem
In England's green and pleasant land.

LITTLE is known about the conditions of bookbinders, apart from their status under the law, prior to 1780. It would appear, however, that the usual working hours had been from six in the morning till nine at night, with only a half an hour's rest for breakfast and one hour's rest for dinner. Any other meal or refreshment having to be taken during the working hours.

In 1747 these hours were worked and the wages of a journeyman were quoted at 12s. 0d. per week. By 1780 a marked improvement had taken place – not only in the price of labour which had risen to 18s. 0d. to £1. 1s. 0d. for journeymen finishers but, through some cause which cannot now be determined, the working hours had been reduced and the time usually worked was from six till eight. Any longer hours being counted as overtime in which case an allowance of bread, cheese and beer was generally made.

According to information now lost the journeymen, shortly before the 1786 strike (which we are now recording), struck for and obtained, the hours eight to nine, which tended to make the employers more fierce against the journeymen when a like demand was a second time made at the above date.

Other evidence would seem to confirm this statement but, on the other hand, John Jaffray – Bookbinder/Historian, had the opinions of some living in his time who had never heard of a strike prior to 1786.

The best evidence we can find shows that in 1780 the hours were generally from six till eight, or twelve-and-a-half working hours to the day, although in some shops there was a custom of employing two sets of men who worked as 'daymen' and 'nightmen', each party working from six till six for the purpose of getting ready by the following morning, or night, such orders as came in by post – mail coaches having not yet been introduced.

For some years prior to 1780 it was the custom of many of the Journeymen to meet in Public Houses adjoining their workshops on Saturday evenings to drink 'a social pint of porter', or pass the time with a 'little harmony', and out of these informal and friendly gatherings, at which a great deal of shop chat was indulged in, grew the first germs of our trade societies.

It was at 'The Cheshire Cheese', Surrey Street, Strand, where some ten or twelve binders met in 1779–80, that the first attempt was made to form a regular society, and on moving to 'The One Tun' in the Strand, near Hungerford Market, in 1780, the Society became established as 'The Friends', and was the centre and origin of the agitation which led up to the strike of 1786. No doubt the long hours of work, which contrasted unfavourably with those of other trades was the principal theme of comment, and a John Lovejoy, later a well known master bookbinder was the first to suggest the desirability of an effort being made to reduce them by one hour by striking.

The idea spread rapidly through the trade and from being much talked about in other meetings, by 1783 a second society was instituted at 'The Green Man' in Bow Street, thereby establishing the first industrial trade society, moving from a social

'Pint of Porter' to discussions of an industrial trade matter, that of course, being illegal at that time.

Between 1783 and 1785, the 'hour' question became a vital affair in trade politics. By this time John Lovejoy, the instigator of the hour, had left the ranks of the Journeymen and had set up in business for himself. A third Society, 'The City Brothers' was also formed with its headquarters at the 'Three Jolly Butchers' in Warwick Lane, near Stationers Hall.

All three Societies charged entrance fees, ranging from a shilling to a guinea, according to the qualifications of the applicant for membership. The entrance money and the weekly subscriptions of a few pence were carefully saved and formed the basis of a Strike Fund. This money was put aside for the period between 1783 and early into 1786 when the Committees of the three Societies met and agreed to take joint action. Their plan was to demand a reduction of one hour from the proprietors of four of the principal shops, and to instruct the journeymen employed in them to give a week's notice if their employers refused the concession.

Representations were accordingly made to the following employers: John Mackinlay, Bow Street; John Jackson, Fountain Court, Strand; John Wingrave, Red Lion Court, Fleet Street; and John Lovejoy, Plough Court, Fetter Lane. It will be remembered that the latter had originally been the prime mover in the hour question. The answer of the four Masters was to discharge all their employees in the hope that the Strike Fund would quickly be dissipated and that the hotheads would come begging for their jobs in a chastened frame of mind. Many of the men, having pocketed a guinea from the Strike Fund, then went on the tramp to the provinces in search of work.

There was not, however, unanimity among the Master Bookbinders in general. Oddly enough, it was George III, the King of England, who was the first employer as a result of a Trade Union Society demand, to grant the hour off the working day. He had a private bindery at Buckingham House and when John Polwarth, his Head Finisher, asked for the reduction, it was given.

John Bell, a well-known publisher and bookseller, whose shop was near the 'Cheshire Cheese' in the Strand, also gave way when approached by Thomas Fairbairn, his Finisher (later to become one of the hostages). The Masters who remained adamant could do nothing against Bell, but they were to have their revenge upon Fairbairn. Several other employers conceded the hour rather than lose their workmen.

James Fraser

The trade was in turmoil, the 'United Friends' called a meeting at the Green Man in Bow Street, which was attended by almost all the journeymen in London, numbering between eighty and a hundred. The result of this meeting was a unanimous resolution to strike – this was at the end of March 1786.

It is difficult to establish a chronological order of events following the resolution to strike. However, to sort the elements of the story in their correct sequence, to the names of Mackinlay, Jackson, Wingrave and Lovejoy (the employers who had been threatened with the departure of their hands if they refused to grant the hour), must be added those of James Fraser of St. Martin's Lane and James Matthews of 18 The Strand.

These six men were apparently the principal members of that group of employers which was long to be known by the journeymen as 'The Prosecuting Masters'.

James Fraser along with Mackinlay and Lovejoy were most determined opponents of the men. Fraser or 'did you never hear of Black Jock, or Blinking Jamie Fraser, who went round about the town to draw the trade together', who had a cast in the eye, was one of the last to see advisability of giving way, though his experience afterwards led him to draw up a 'Plan and Journeyman Bookbinders' which our illustration represents him as holding.

Following as many as eighty journeymen being dismissed throughout the trade, the Masters proposed to prosecute twenty-four of them, all finishers. On Tuesday, 25th April, 1786, they were indicted at the Middlesex New Sessions House in Clerkenwell, commonly known as Hicks Hall. The application for the indictment was made with the minimum of fuss and publicity, in the hope that as many of the men as possible could be clapped into gaol before bail could be found.

The Indictment was an exceedingly lengthy document full of legal repetition. It is not worth copying the Indictment in full but here is the principal count:

> *Middlesex. The Jurors for Our Lord the King upon their Oath present that Thomas Armstronge, Mungo Hall, Paul Isaac Rockey, Jacob Brown, William Dukeys, John Townley, William Craig, William Graham, John Lightbody, Joseph Scott, William Lewis, William Lilbourne, Thomas Ashman, William Wood, Thomas Fairbairn, John Heeley, Alexander Greig, Thomas Marshall, Watkin Nimmo, Edward Ferguson, John George, John Shields, Alexander Hogg, and Thomas Fife, all late of The Parish of St. Paul, Covent Garden, Labourers; being evil disposed persons, and workmen and journeymen in the art and mystery and manual occupation of bookbinders, and not content to work and labour in that art and mystery by the usual number of hours in each day, and at the usual rate and prices for which they and other workmen and journeymen in the same art and mystery were used and had been accustomed to work and labour, but devising and intending to take from lessen and diminish one hour in each day's work, and to compel their respective masters and employers to pay them the same price for each day's work, so diminished by one hour, as though they had worked the usual number of hours in each day, and thereby to enhance the price of their and other workmen and journeymen's wages in the same art and mystery on the 22nd day of March in the 26th Geo. III . . . did unlawfully conspire, combine, confederate, and agree together to take from lessen and diminish one hour in each day's work . . . and afterwards on the same day did unlawfully assemble and meet together and form themselves into an unlawful Society to support each other in such unlawful purpose . . . (and that they agreed) that they and each and every of them would not work or labour any longer for their respective masters and employers . . . to the great damage and oppression not only of their several masters and employers, but also of divers others of the liege subjects of our said Lord the King, his crown and dignity . . . and being not content to work and labour in that art and mystery by the usual number of hours in each day – being twelve hours and one half in each day – did conspire, combine, confederate, and agree together to lessen the hours by one, and . . . that if their respective masters and employers refused to comply with such unlawful terms, that they and every of them would leave their respective employments . . . and that these twenty-four did entice others to leave and did covenant and agree to support such other who would leave.*

William Hall (Strike Committee Member) recalled in his 84th year:

> "An old man named Nimmo, who had been long in London, prying about got notice of the indictment. He gave notice to the men. Not knowing who were indicted, they left town in parties, meeting at Kensington Gravel Pits (Notting Hill Gate) at an Inn where they spent the night. Sunday morning, old Nimmo, who was very useful to the men, brought a list of the twenty-four indicted men, being those who had struck from the four shops. On Monday morning they were bailed by the Justice in Bow Steet by different men in

sixes. T. Armstronge and I, with four others, got Mr. John Bell and John Withers (Landlord of the 'Green Man') for bail. Bell's foreman, Fairbairn, having got Bell to give the hour, the Masters got him pushed in amongst the twenty-four indicted."

The New Sessions House, Clerkenwell

During the few days following their indictment, the men and their friends did their best to procure bail, and by Monday May 1st, they succeeded and were all bailed in groups of six before the Justice at Bow Street.

Mr John Bell, who had given the hour, and Mr John Withers, Landlord of 'The Green Man' in Bow Street, appeared as bail for one party of six, amongst whom were Armstronge and Hall, two of Mackinlay's men, and Fairbourne, Mr Bell's finisher, who had been included in the charge but who had continued to work for Mr Bell until he went up for sentence.

Overleaf is a copy of one of the bail papers.

The Trial

The journeymen obtained the services of Thomas Erskine, a well-known advocate for skilled legal assistance, for their defence. His Brief was marked 15 guineas (the Masters had also sought to employ him). The men briefed William Garrow as well, at a fee of 10 guineas, and their third Counsel, who received 5 guineas, was one Sylvester, later Recorder of London.

There was a succession of delays before the trial finally took place. Erskine succeeded in having the case transferred from the General Sessions to the Court of King's Bench. It was to have been heard by Lord Justice Mansfield on the 3rd November, 1786, but was postponed and it finally came before Judges Ashurst, Buller and Grosse in the February of 1787.

Middlesex } To all Constables, Headboroughs and
to wit others of His Majesties Officers of
the Peace for the said County whom
it may concern.

Whereas William Graham hath this day found sufficient
sureties before me, Sir Sampson Wright, Knt., one of His
Majesties Justices of the Peace for the said County, for
his personal appearance at the next General Sessions
of Oyer and Terminer to be holden at the New Sessions
House in and for the said County; then and there to plead
to a certain indictment for unlawfully conspiring,
combining, confederating, and agreeing with divers other
persons, being workmen and journeymen in the art, mystery
and manual occupation of bookbinders, to take from, lessen
and diminish one hour in each day from the usual number
of hours which they and other workmen and journeymen
in the first art were accustomed to work and labour and to
compel their respective masters and employers in the same
art to pay them the same prices for each days work so
diminished by one hour, as they had worked the usual
number of hours. To which indictment they have not yet
appeared or pleaded.
These are therefore in His Majesties name to
charge and command you and every of you immediately
on sight hereof, not to arrest, imprison, molest, or any
otherwise detain the body of the said William Graham
for by reason or means of the Act above mentioned
and no other. And this shall be to you each and every
of you a sufficient warrant. Given under my hand and
seal the first day of May in the year of Our Lord
1786
Sampson Wright.

William Graham Bail Paper.

6

Although efforts were made to interest the general public in the journeymen bookbinders' cause, it was said that the dispute received little enough attention, even though notices were printed entitled 'To the Public' in the papers *Morning Herald* and *The Gazeteer,* the latter on 6th April, 1786 and the former on 9th May, 1786, the text of which survives today.

During the ten months that this charge of conspiracy had been hanging over their heads, great feelings of bitterness had grown up against John Lovejoy (one of the Prosecuting Masters) for it was he who, as a journeyman himself at the time, had initiated in 1783 the campaign for the reduction of the hour. When he had been one of their number none was such a stickler for upholding their rights and privileges. Indeed, he once informed them that 'when he died they would call him their father and even revere his memory'. A few years later his very presence on earth was unwelcome.

As William Hall recalled in his writings on the event of the trial:

> Expecting every day the trial would come on, some of the youths bought a halter and made it up into a parcel, sending it to Lovejoy, with a note they put in, and desired him to make use of it.
>
> The Committee was sitting at the Coffee House near the Westminster Hall. Old man Nimmo told me that Lovejoy had got the halter. He said: 'If you will give me a bottle of brandy or rum, I will bring it to you'. He went to the Hall with his bottle and glass, and got a few Masters together, with Lovejoy among them, pretending to be very friendly with them, and that he had got a bottle to treat them to a glass. Squeezing in beside Lovejoy, giving him the bottle and glass he took care to get the halter from his pocket, and brought it to the Committee, who soon burnt it, sending word to Erskine, who was our Leading Counsel, letting him know we had got it. The trial is now going on. An old man called Judge Ashurst was trying the case; the Counsellors busy examining the prosecutors. On Lovejoy's turn he made a great flourish, telling the Judge and Jury that the men had used him very ill, realting the story of the halter. Erskine says: 'Now Mr Lovejoy, you have been telling a cock and bull story to injure these honest men; will you be so good as to show my Lord Judge and Jury this said halter?' He put his hand first in one pocket and then in the other, but no halter could be found there. 'My Lord Judge, is that man proper to appear as a witness in any trial?' There was a general laughter in the court, and Lovejoy was dismissed in disgrace.

It was a pity that old Nimmo never went into the witness box, for he would have undoubtedly provided further light relief. He seems to have acted as a spy for the journeymen in the Master Bookbinders' Camp, for the latter even intended to call him to testify on their behalf. William Hall remembered:

> An anecdote tells of the 'practical joke' which was intended to have been played upon 'Old Judge Ashurst' by Nimmo . . . who, by the way, made a very profitable speculation by selling nuts at Westminster Hall on one or more of the occasions that general meetings of idle, curious or anxious binders were held there. The men, in order to show the laborious nature of their trade and the reasonableness of their demand for reduced hours of work, intended to have shown in court a heavy beating hammer, and as

Nimmo expected to be called as a witness against them, it was arranged that he should exhibit one of sixteen pounds weight from Wingraves where Lilburne worked. He was to have made 'very light of it', and endeavour to persuade Ashurst to inspect it for himself and to contrive to drop it on the 'old rogue's' toes, as if by accident. Not having been called as a witness, however, prevented the consequences of such a serious calamity.

The Hostages

No contemporary account of the remainder of the proceedings survived. Probably eighteen of the twenty-four defendants were discharged 'sine die', while the remaining six, known to be the ringleaders, were bound over, with instructions to return to work or suffer the consequences. It is likely that the Prosecuting Masters, at one point or other during the trial, instructed their Counsel not to press too hardly for a conviction, as by that time they were heartily tired of the whole affair, and were prepared to grant the hour rather than protract the struggle. In addition it was preferable have the men working in their shops rather than sitting in gaol.

It was thought that six hostages, threatened with imprisonment, would provide security for the good behaviour of the eighteen others. Their names were: Armstronge, 'Master' Mackinlay; Craig, 'Master' Jackson; Lilburne, 'Master' Wingrave; Wood, 'Master' Mathews; Fairbairn, 'Master' Bell; and Hogg, 'Master' Lovejoy.

Thomas Fairbairn, in fact, had never struck work at all, but was forced in under the charge of conspiracy by the Prosecuting Masters to spite John Bell, who had granted the hour without argument. All the men were Finishers.

Upon Erskine's advice, the Strike Committee then immediately dissolved itself. If trade meetings were held, then it was in secret. Three of the hostages remained on strike. Fairbairn continued to work for Bell and Wood had set up in business for himself shortly after the strike had begun. Hogg may have returned to Lovejoy as he subsequently escaped punishment, either because he was at work, or on account of Lovejoy's poor display in the witness box.

It is impossible not to admire the firmness and constancy of the six who thus calmly awaited the penalties of the law.

They knew they were liable to imprisonment, the pillory, or the loss of an ear, yet believing in the righteousness of their cause, they persisted in refusing to obey the Judges.

Tuesday 8th May 1787 was an anxious day for the binders of London. Once more they assembled in Westminster Hall and the hostages were brought up at the Court of King's Bench, when on the Judge's learning they had not obeyed the mandate of the court, five of them were sentenced to two years' imprisonment in Newgate.

The following account of the case is taken from *The Morning Chronicle and London Advertiser* of Friday May 11th 1787:

> On Tuesday, the Journeymen bookbinders were brought up before the Judges of the Kings Bench, in order to receive judgement, they have been convicted of conspiracy against their masters, by demanding of them an abridgement of their hours of labour, and leaving their employ when refused. The Judges on the Bench were Messrs. Ashurst, Buller and Grosse, who upon this and former occasions, on this cause, acted with the greatest impartiality, and at the same time showed a proper resentment against such daring attacks upon the liberty of the state and the laws of constitution.

Mr Justice Ashurst took the lead in the business, made many trite and judicious observations, and very candidly spoke of the lenity of the masters towards their Journeymen, there having been twenty four convicted, and only five of them, at the request of their counsel to the masters, received as hostages for the rest.

The sentence passed upon them was two years imprisonment in Newgate, which the wise and learned Judge could not think too severe, in order to check the growing evils of combinations in a trading and free country.

The counsel for the prosecution were Messrs. Bearcroft and Minger. Attorney E. Naylor, Great Newport Street.

The counsel for the defendants, Messrs. Erskine and Garrow.

The masters who were present still possessing the same feelings of humanity, were shocked to think that the misguided zeal of the body at large, should be so severely felt by a few individuals. It is to be hoped that this sentence will be a warning to artificers in general, and prove a means of their avoiding such combinations in future.

The wise and learned Judge did 'not think the sentence severe', and we are at a loss to understand why the masters should be 'shocked', for the state of feeling at the time regarding the punitive powers of the Judges was callous in the extreme.

Those were days when the public generally agreed in the policy of avenging crime, and looked unmoving upon batches of 30 to 40 miserable wretches paying the penalty for minor offences by death upon an open scaffold at the close of each sessions. In the previous month of the same year it was recorded that the Sheriff of London had 'given orders for the building of twenty four pillories, as it is expected this term will furnish more tenants for the exalted buildings than ever known in the memory of man.'

The pillory and the gallows were regarded as other public sports, for the people had not awakened to the savagery of their laws, and the debasing effect of such exhibitions. It was still thought necessary that some should suffer that others might be saved.

Sentence of two years' imprisonment having been passed by Judge Ashurst, the five 'Martyrs' were taken to Newgate Prison where they contrived to make themselves as comfortable as possible.

In 1816 Robert Pratt, a journeyman, wrote a 'Narrative of the Rise and Progress of the Bookbinders Society', which was prepared for the Anniversary Dinner of Lodge No. 4 in the latter year. No copy survives, but the 'Friendly Finishers Circular' contains the following extract from it.

No sooner had our friends been conveyed to prison than the journeymen felt a new ardour in the cause. They immediately determined to allow each sufferer a guinea per week, but the difficulty was to obtain supplies for this purpose.

Persons were appointed to attend the various shops weekly, and it will astonish the bookbinders of the present day (here we are talking about 1787) to hear that nearly two thousand pounds were obtained to support the men and defray the law expenses.

Not only did the trade contribute a certain weekly quota, but other trades, stimulated by the fortitude they could not fail to admire, stepped forward with their contributions. Nay, such was the enthusiasm of the time, that females connected with the trade contributed very handsomely to the general cause.

Newgate Gaol Yard

The five 'Martyrs', being in a position to pay for a modicum of comfort, were not locked up with the common felons in Newgate, they shared a room of their own, within the 'state side' of Newgate – 'where there were no restrictions as to hours or beer'.

Robert Pratt, indicated that when he was a lad he often visited them and sometimes even slept in their room. He stated that 'besides the guinea per week which the imprisoned men received, their families were well supplied with presents. The men themselves were daily visited in Newgate by binders and others – the liquor drunk on such occasions would come to no small amount'.

Another veteran told John Jaffray, that in those days there was a tap room in Newgate Prison and they that got in might sit there and get as full as they liked.

John Jaffray in 1845 also wrote:

> The rigours of their confinement – if the many anecdotes still in existence relating thereunto to be credited – were mitigated in as great a degree as could be accomplished by friends and well-wishers

outside the walls of Newgate. Legs of mutton, ribs of beef, gallons of beer, bottles of gin, and friendly balls, each in turn assisted to cheer them in their captivity. Indeed, it has been asserted by old friends that the substantial gifts thus presented to them and their families were so numerous as to admit of, at least, more than one victim saving the whole of the guinea per week allowed them.

The Death of a Victim and Free Pardon

The men had not long been in prison before 'a coldness arose between William Wood and the others, and it was thought, or at least said, that if he had "lushed" (drank) like them he would not have died.' It is possible that he was not only sensitive to his surroundings and the rough humour of his companions, but in poor physical shape as well. He caught what was known as 'gaol fever', or distemper, a disease which destroyed 'more individuals in prison than were publicly killed by the Hangman', old chronicles record many instances of its ravages, and even as late as 1750, on one occasion 'the Lord Mayor, one Alderman, two Judges, the greater part of the Jury, and a number of the spectators, caught the jail distemper' while at the Old Bailey and died. After only a few days illness poor Wood died in the arms of his wife – on the 10th March, 1788.

William Hall, a member of the Strike Committee, wrote an account of his funeral:

> There was a very large concourse of people attended his funeral, which came down Newgate, along Fleet Street and the Strand, coming opposite Mr Matthews' house. Mrs Matthews, Wood's aunt, was standing looking through their dining room window. The corpse was lowered to the flags with a heavy groan. Mrs Matthews was observed to fall down – it was supposed she fainted at the sight, as they were somehow the cause of his imprisonment (Matthews being one of the Prosecuting Masters). The funeral was brought round this way instead of going up Holborn, the nearest way.

The 'nearest way' was to the 'Wesleyan Chapel in Tottenham Court Road.'

The four survivors remained in prison. When they had been at Newgate for close on twelve months, to use William Hall's words, 'some new Sheriff came on'. He continued:

> It is the Sheriff's business to visit the prisons along with the keepers, each of them a week in their turn. Coming around the first time with the keeper of the prison, a Sheriff Bloxham when he came to the binders' room – saw the room, the men all clean, well dressed, a good joint roasting at the fire – he stood with surprise, saying to the keeper, 'WHAT MEN ARE THESE? THEY NEVER CAN BE FELONS.' HE ANSWERED HIM, 'THEY ARE THE BOOKBINDERS FOR COMBINATION'. 'WHAT THE BOOKBINDERS HERE STILL? I THOUGHT THEY HAD BEEN LIBERATED LONG SINCE. BY YOUR APPEAR-ANCE YOU MUST HAVE MANY FRIENDS OUT OF DOORS. GET A PETITION MADE OUT, SIGNED BY AS MANY RESPECTABLE PEOPLE YOU CAN; BRING IT TO ME, YOU SHALL NOT BE MUCH LONGER HERE – I AM A BOOKBINDER MYSELF.'

This was done, and Sheriff Bloxham presented the petition to Lord Sydney, then Secretary of State, requesting the release of the men. It would appear, however, that Lord Sydney had laid the petition aside and forgotten it, at least no further notice was taken of its prayer until after a few weeks delay the Sheriff again visited the Prison, when he was surprised to find the men still imprisoned. He thereupon called for a hackney coach and went directly to the office of the Secretary of State and so effectually pleaded the men's cause that a free pardon was granted them.

Sheriff Bloxham's intervention did not come like a bolt from the blue, he had been carefully primed by Mr Trueman, 'The Friendly Barber' who attended him professionally. Truman was acquainted with both Armstrong and Fairbairn, two of the victims. Indeed, it is possible that he sometimes came to Newgate prison to serve them.

There is no doubt that Trueman discussed the men's plight with the Sheriff, and that Bloxham felt a degree of sympathy towards individuals of a trade so closely allied to his own. He was even good enough to pay the gaol fees demanded upon their release, which took place on 28th June, 1788, some fourteen months after the trial.

During the next day or two the martyrs rode around the town in coaches and, accompanied by four or five 'respected members of the trade' . . . waited on their fellow tradesmen for the purpose of returning thanks for the attentions paid to them during their confinement.

William Hall recollected that 'when the men were liberated there was no public dinner or procession, but a burst of congratulations, a general feeling of social joy, such as I have never experienced before or since'.

All were anxious to get the men into work and it is known that the 'Prosecuting Masters' made no difficulties for them. THE HATCHET WAS BURIED.

Commemoration

It is of some interest in ending this brief account of our beginning with an account of the story concerning miniature portraits painted in honour of the martyrs, and of the foundation of the Anniversary Dinner.

Shortly after their release, the members of Lodge No. 1 subscribed for and commissioned 'Munro, a very excellent portrait painter' to paint miniatures of each of the martyrs. They were executed on ivory tablets 'about the size of a couple of crown pieces', and cost 10 guineas the lot.

The miniatures were not presented to the men, whose deeds they commemorated, but remained the property of the Lodge. The tablets were inserted into gilt metal frames, about an inch in breadth, studded with glass or paste, and with four projecting rays. Each was attached to a ribbon, about four inches wide, richly embroidered with coloured silk and gold lace.

Officially known as 'Regalias', these decorations were commonly described as 'Horse Collars'. They were worn on lodge nights and other special occasions by the President, Vice President, Secretary and other Officers of the Lodge.

In 1794, Thomas Fairbairn had a violent quarrel with Thomas Faulkner, then one of the leading lights in the Trade Society, and resigned his membership in a pique. The members of No. 1 Lodge were so incensed that they took his portrait from its frame and publicly burned it in a tobacco pipe. It was said that when he later made his peace and rejoined the Society, his picture was once again limned and restored to its place of honour.

In 1845, when John Jaffray was asking the veterans for information about them, the old 'Regalias' had disappeared. Some thought that they had been lost after an Anniversary Dinner, or left in pledge to a landlord for refreshments supplied; others that they had been pawned by a Lodge Secretary who was short of cash. Whatever the answer, there is little likelihood of their ever coming to light, it would have been pleasant to have been able to reproduce the portraits for the 200-year anniversary.

The Anniversary

In 1784, the United Friendly Society of Journeymen Bookbinders' consisting of four lodges, issued its first printed book of rules. The eighth article stated 'That our Annual Festival be held on 28th June, to commemorate the liberation of our friends. The stewards are to be chosen by ballot, on refusal to serve shall be fined two shillings and six pence each.'

The first dinner was held in 1790, and was organised by Lodge 1 as a private affair. General Trade Dinners did not take place until after 1794. The minutes relating to the celebration of 1799 survive.

FRIENDLY SOCIETY ANNIVERSARY
HELD AT
MR. ARAM'S, MONTPELIER GARDENS, WALWORTH,
28th JUNE, 1799

The Friendly Sire (Chairman) and Officers took their respective seats near four o'clock, and partook of an excellent Dinner. After that the Friendly Sire proceeded to conduct the remaining part of the day with the usual order, which gave the utmost satisfaction from all parts of the room. Mr. Lovejoy, a visiting master, seemed pleased with the order and regulations of the day, and proposed that the Stewards' health should be drunk, followed with three cheers. The usual ceremonies being over, after Dinner the Friends dispersed to their different recreations until supper time, when they returned to the room for supper, which was done with quietness. After that the friends returned to their different habitations.

Browning, Friendly Sire, Neal, Past Friendly Sire, Tomlinson, Secretary (Mackinlay's head Finisher). Visitors: Messrs. Craig, Armstrong ('Victims,' now employers), Mackinlay, Lovejoy, Hering, Brook, Timbury (bookbinders' brass tool engraver), Wright, Poole, Egleton, McNair, Armstrong at the Palace (the superintendent of the Royal Bindery), Stevenson, Trueman (the 'Friendly Barber'), Tapper, Neale of Lodge 4, and Clarke.'

The amazing situation at this Anniversary Dinner was the fact that John Lovejoy, the leading Prosecution Master, seems to have been the Guest of Honour, whereas twelve years previously they would have liked to have hung him.

The Anniversary was still celebrated as late as the end of the nineteenth century, although by that date participants appeared to talk more of latter day strikes than that of 1786.

The Six Hostages (later the Martyrs)

8th May, 1787 – Sentenced to two years' imprisonment, except Hogg, who was released by Judge Ashurst and others at Westminster Hall.

Committed to Newgate Prison for close on fourteen months. As a result of a petition by Sheriff Bloxham and following a free pardon and payment of gaol fees demanded upon their release, they were released on 28th June, 1788.

Thomas Armstronge   Master – John Mackinlay
Born: Hexham, Northumberland

William Craig   Master – John Jackson
Born: Berwick-on-Tweed,
Northumberland

William Lilburne   Master – John Wingrave
Born: Carnew in Co. Wickford,
Ireland

William Wood   Master – James Mathews
Born: Oxford, Oxfordshire

Died in prison (Gaol Fever)

Thomas Fairbairn   Master – John Bell
Born: Edinburgh, Scotland

Alexander Hogg   Master – John Lovejoy

Prosecuting Masters

John Mackinlay   Bow Street, London

John Jackson   Fountain Court, Strand, London

John Wingrave   Red Lion Court, Fleet Street, London

John Lovejoy   Plough Court, Fetter Lane, London

James Fraser   St. Martin's Lane, London

James Matthews   18 The Strand, London

2

The 'Dons' and the 'Clean Shirt Boys'

Brothers all, with hearts united,
Lend a helping, willing hand;
Extend our cause! you are invited,
Spread our precepts through the land.

THE earliest known laws must have been a revised code adopted by the Lodges during the year 1793, in order to meet the requirements of an additional Lodge founded in that year.

Prior to that date it was the rule that Lodges should be composed of not more than fifty, but as the members had been actively organising, some of the Lodges became overfilled; this happened in Lodge II, held at the 'Jolly Butchers', in Warwick-lane, where most of the city men met – they were consequently nicknamed 'Butcher' – when Mr Thos W. Faulkner began, about 1792, to establish a new Lodge.

With the assistance of Mr D. Dobell, this became an accomplished fact on the night of 1st July 1793, when forty-six founders registered their names on the books of Lodge IV, at the 'Cheshire Cheese', Chapter House-court, St. Paul's Churchyard. Shortly afterwards it was removed to the 'George', in Little Drury-lane, where it became the next in importance to Lodge I – 'The Dons', – being the general House of Call for the trade, and meeting-place for the Trade Committees; owing to the respectability of its members, who at that time wore knee breeches and white stockings, it was known as 'The White Stocking Lodge'.

The members of Lodge III were known as 'The Clean Shirt Boys' because 'few of them could boast of the possession of one on Monday mornings', but their numbers were not so strong as those of other Lodges.

In order to understand the constitution of the Society which was evidently only a blind – appended is the full text of the

ARTICLES

'Art. 1. – The business of the Society shall be regulated by three officers, elected by ballot. The first bearing the title of Friendly Sire, the second that of Friend Secretary, the third that of Friend Assistant-Secretary. The officers elected for the first two quarters after the Anniversary, to fill the office fourteen weeks, the last two quarters twelve weeks.

N.B. – The past Friendly to be deemed an officer for the instruction of new ones. He is likewise to keep a book to receive fines and entries, and keep a clear account thereof. The Secretary is to keep proper minutes of each night's meeting. The Assistant Secretary to receive each night's payments.

'Art. 2. – Any member present refusing to stand when elected, "If out of office six months", or not having paid his fine within that time, shall be fined one shilling.

'Art. 3. – That the officers shall attend, and be entrusted with their respective Regalias, at half-past eight o'clock, on default thereof to be fined one shilling, "except they send their key and a proper apology." Should any officer be absent, the Friendly Sire shall have full power to nominate whom he pleases to fill the office for that night. On refusal, the Friend appointed shall be fined one shilling, exclusive of any other article. N.B. – The Lodge to close precisely at eleven o'clock, unless business requires it longer.

'Art. 4. – That proper respect shall be paid to the Chair, any Friend refusing to obey the F.S. when called to order, or otherwise insulting him in Lodge hours, or insulting any member individually, or the members in general, shall be fined one shilling.

'Art. 5. – That this Society shall meet every Monday fortnight, each member to pay fourpence to be spent, and fourpence towards an Anniversary Dinner to be held on the 28th of June. Should the 28th fall upon a Sunday, it shall then be kept on the Saturday prior. The stewards for conducting it shall be chosen by ballot. If they decline the office when chosen, to be fined two shillings and sixpence. No person to receive a dinner ticket unless he is full on the book on the night the tickets are issued, and of which the F.S. is to give due notice on the night prior, and no tickets transferable.

'Art. 6. – Any member who does not appear on the night prior to the quarterly night, he shall be summoned by the Secretary to clear his book on the quarterly night, and for which the Secretary shall receive twopence for each summons, and for each neglect he shall be fined sixpence.

'Art. 7. – Any person wishing to become a member of this Society, must be proposed one night before he can be admitted, and if his character appears respectable, he may then be balloted for, and made in the usual form, by the payment of five shillings. The time of payment not to exceed three months from the date of entry. All arrears of the feast-money to be paid, and the proposer to pay one shilling if the proposed does not come forward.

'Art. 8. – No member shall be entitled to vote on the night of his admission; nor any person again received, who does not take leave 'personally, or by proxy,' delivered to the Secretary of the Society, on the first meeting night after he leaves the town, without being entered on the books as a new member.

'Art. 9. – That every member shall attend on the night of the election, or send his ballot, intimating the Friends he wishes to fill the respective offices, in default thereof to fine one shilling, and for not clearing the book sixpence, and if not cleared on the night after the quarter he shall be expelled.

'Art. 10. – Notice of the election night to be given in the Lodge by the F.S. on the night prior.

'Art. 11. – All motions of a general nature to be made on the night following the election night, and given in writing to the F.S., and on no other night. Any Friend making use of illiberal language, or insinuating anything prejudicial to the character of a brother member, without sufficient proof, shall, on conviction thereof, be fined, or expelled, as the majority think the case may require.

'Art. 12. – That each Lodge be limited to the number of fifty. The entrance-money to be equally divided in the four Lodges by the report of the Secretaries' entry books once a quarter. Should the Lodges amount to more than fifty, each Lodge in rotation shall admit one. Any member who is transferred from one Lodge to another, shall give information and take honourable leave prior to joining another, in order that the person coming from either of the four Lodges, with evidence to give or receive, may transfer their feast-money at the same time. No member to take leave but on a quarterly night.

'Art. 13. – The F.S. shall not suffer any profane language to be used without a severe reprimand for such depravity of conduct. Any member entering the Lodge-room disguised in liquor, and being troublesome, the F.S. shall order him to withdraw, in order that moderation, decency, and good sense be the leading features of each night's meeting.

'Art. 14. – That no member shall plead ignorance of the above articles, they shall be read every quarterly night immediately following the minutes, and all fines to go to the box –

'God Save the King'

A few old minutes which still remain, on loose various sized sheets of paper, shew the usual order of conducting the business of the Lodges, while from other sources the harmonious character of the after proceedings are drawn.

At half-past eight the Friendly Sire and other officers were invested with their regalias, and having taken their places, the Lodge was opened by the F.S. calling 'Attention'. The minutes of the previous meeting were then read, new members admitted, trade business discussed, defaulting members erased, loans or gifts to other trades granted, and loans to members granted upon the security of two other members.

If there was no other business the F.S. would then say, 'Friends, there being no other business before the Chair, I declare the Lodge closed. We will now proceed to harmony.' Jugs of porter were then brought in and circulated, while tobacco was served from underneath the table, where it was usually kept in the Vice President's hat, both being paid for by the fourpences contributed by the members.

Bowls of negus or punch were also frequent after the conclusion of the business in prosperous times, and it was common for members taking honourable leave to give five shilling or more for the others to drink their health, on which occasion the Lodge usually added a like amount.

At eleven o'clock the proceedings ended, a list of those present being taken and placed upon the minutes, which usually wound up with remarks such as the following: 'There being no other business, the remainder of the night was spent with the greatest friendship, and at eleven o'clock the Lodge closed'; 'After spending an agreeable evening, the Lodge closed in good harmony', 'No other business of importance occurred; the Lodge closed with that degree of conviviality, harmony, and good order for which the members of Lodge I, have hitherto been distinguished.'

No wonder the members of Lodge I, were called 'The Dons'!

Looking carefully through the foregoing 'Articles', we find there is no intimation of any general body such as a Trade Committee, or payments to men out of work, or of funds for general trade purposes; the whole business set forth indicates a friendly meeting only, with the main object of an anniversary dinner; and in the few remaining minutes of the meetings there are but few and slight indications of any business affecting the working of the trade.

But the fines were plentiful enough, and as there is no direction as to their use after they had gone 'to the box', we may fairly assume that 'the box' was the war chest of the trade, and the fines made up a fund from which all expenses incurred for trade purposes were drawn.

Roger Payne, known as 'the father of English bookbinding', pictured here in 1817.

That there were committees from the Amalgamated Lodges is also certain from existing minutes, and doubtlessly upon trade matters, for in one we read that 'Friend Tomlinson, as secy. to the meeting of oficers of the four Lodges (held at the George little Drury lane) read the resulutions of the meting.'

The laws forbidding trade combinations account for these otherwise strange omissions, but did not prevent the active though secret work of organisation and discussion of trade grievances, which had become very plentiful.

The trade was overrun with apprentices, a serious sub-division of labour had been commenced that threatened the livings of men who had hitherto been used to preform the whole of the work, and, what was almost as fatal to their well-being, the number of small master-men increased rapidly, and with them the evil of assistance by their wives and children in times of brisk trade, instead of that of properly qualified workmen.

Under these circumstances, towards the close of 1793 the trade was again in a state of ferment, not because the trade was slack and employment scarce – fortunately, few of those who could and would work were unemployed, indeed, it was no uncommon occurrence for employers to give a man half-a-guinea to induce him to go to work.

An early bookbinders' membership card.

'There has been a wonderful increase in business that had kept pace with the augmentation of members', and the time was judged to be favourable for a determined effort to put down the abuses which had grown up during the partial prostration which followed the strike of 1786.

Since that time the masters' Society had been dissolved, but late in the year 1793 or very early in 1794 it was re-formed and a Committee appointed to prepare a new and increased list of prices for binding to be submitted to the booksellers and publishers.

This was just the opportunity that the men needed, and it was seized upon by the leading spirits of the time, to the ultimate advantage of the trade.

About the middle of February in the year 1794, the first movement towards a further reduction of the hours of labour was made in a conversation between Mr Thomas W. Faulkner and Mr Burnett, two of the members of Lodge IV. Mr Faulkner had learnt from three of the employers, Messrs. J. Millar, Crawford, and J. Anderson, that the Masters' Society had been reformed with the intention of a general rise of prices for their work, and he suggested that it was a favourable opportunity to obtain a reduction of one hour per day for the journeymen. Burnett agreed with the idea and promised his assistance. Faulkner next consulted Mr T. Armstrong, one of the victims of 1786–87, but his opinion was 'however much I wish it, I can give you no hope'. Nothing daunted, however, Faulkner and Burnett took an early opportunity of addressing their Lodge upon the question, and succeeded not only in obtaining its approval, but the appointment of a committee of three, consisting of Faulkner, Burnett, and Gould, with the understanding that the other Lodges should be invited to co-operate with them. Mr Faulkner then wrote the other Lodges, who responded to the call by each appointing three representatives, making in all a committee of twelve, who met for the first time early in March at the 'George', in Little Drury-lane, when Mr Faulkner was elected president. The first question of importance was the mode of proceeding. Faulkner's advice, according to his own account of the movement, was 'to open a correspondence with the employers, and then act according to circumstances.' This met with the approbation of the committee, and Faulkner wrote 'congratulating them upon the occasion, and wishing them success. This had the desired effect. We received an answer thanking us for our good wishes and expressing their expectation of receiving an advance of price at no distant period. I then wrote again to them expressing our satisfaction, at the same time hoping that on such an occasion somewhat would be done for the benefit of the journeymen – stating that previous to a final arrangement with the booksellers for prices, it was but just that they should be acquainted with our desires. I wrote the masters several times, and about the middle of April was informed that they had a plan for the benefit of the men. I wrote and requested to be put in possession of their plan. It was this: when a man of good character died, his widow should receive assistance from the masters. This I objected to immediately, observing that merit should be rewarded whilst it could be enjoyed; and gave notice that one hour's reduction from our daily labour was what we expected.' A conference was requested by the masters' committee and agreed to, when the four deemed most efficient – Faulkner, Burnett, Poole and Gould – were appointed to meet the employers and negotiate with them on behalf of the trade. They met at the 'Cheshire Cheese' by St. Dunstan's, on 1st May, Faulkner taking the leading part for the men, and Mr J. Tuck, president of the Masters' Society, for the employers, but no decision was come to upon the question of reduced time, and the meeting was adjourned upon the understanding that the proceedings should be kept secret on both sides. Faulkner complained that this compact was not adhered to by the employers, for on the same evening, after the conference, they reported the whole case to their Society. Some general remarks of his thus reported were taken as applying to Mr Lewis, his employer, and in consequence a resolution was passed that no further communication with the men's committee should take place while Faulkner remained a member thereof. His complaint seems an unreasonable one, except in so far as it was justifiable on account of having been falsely reported, for however much it may have been advisable on the men's part to abstain from giving particulars of a conference where nothing was determined, but where they had nothing to give away or lose, – on the other hand it was absolutely necessary that the sub-committee should inform their full body what the men desired and the reasons for the request. But Mr Faulkner, in spite of the good services he rendered the trade, was an autocrat who could understand no side other than his own, and who would brook no opposition from whatever source.

The sudden break-down of the negotiations brought matters to a climax, for the men were determined to force their demand, and the employers, expecting a struggle, bound themselves, under an agreement imposing a penalty of £50, not to give the hour. A meeting of the whole trade was called without delay, and held at the 'Robin Hood,' New-street-square. After the position had been explained,

J. Faulkner – brother of the leader of the movement – rose and declared that he should ask his employer for the hour on the following Saturday. The idea was quickly taken up by one and another, who rose and expressed their intentions in the same form, until the whole meeting had decided, without any advice from the committee, upon that line of action. The chairman even warned those present that 'it was not the advice from the chair, but every man, individually, had a right to stipulate upon what terms he would sell his labour and abilities to another'. On the following Saturday the hour was everywhere asked for, but without success, the general answer being 'I will consider it'; Faulkner was discharged, Mr Lewis being incensed against him for his remarks at the conference, but he was the only man who suffered in consequence of this action.

After a short pause, during which everything looked very discouraging, Faulkner conceived the idea of starting a co-operative bindery and appealing to the publishers for work, but the Society was without any appreciable amount of funds, there being only a little more than £20 in hand between the four Lodges. In order to carry out his plan, Faulkner applied to a friend, Mr Shepherd, a tax collector, of Chiswell-street, who agreed to advance the money necessary on the security of Mr Faulkner, and an order was at once given to Mullins the press maker for standing-presses and thirty lying-presses, upon the condition that it was not to be proceeded with until after the last day of May, when, if the hour was granted, the order might be cancelled. The news of this movement was industriously circulated, and came upon the employers just as they received the publishers' reply to their own demand, which was, that rather than pay any additional price for their work, they would take on men and have it all done indoors. This double difficulty created no little consternation in their ranks; to be foiled in the effort for an advance of prices was bad enough, but the threatened loss of work was more serious, and another meeting was called to take into consideration this new aspect of the question. A compromise with the men was suggested, with the rescinding of the resolution of non-intercourse; a course strongly opposed by Lovejoy, the former companion of 'The Friends' and instigator of the strike in 1786 – now known amongst the journeymen as 'The Tyrant' – but it was nevertheless carried, and an invitation was sent to the men's committee to meet Mr Tuck and Mr Wingrave at Lovell's-court, Paternoster-row, where Mr Tuck carried on business. At this juncture Mr Gould retired from the men's committee, and Mr D. Dobell, who worked for Lovejoy, was appointed in his place. The meeting resulted in formulating the basis of an agreement that the employers on their part would give the hour on the Michaelmas day next ensuing, provided that the men would refuse to work for any employer who did not belong to the Masters' Society; the employer to contribute towards any expenses incurred through drawing men out to enforce this agreement.

A general meeting of the men was called in June, at the 'One Tun,' Strand, when the committee's agreement was ratified, though not without considerable dissatisfaction being expressed by those who worked for binders unconnected with the Masters' Society; of these malcontents Mr Faulkner made short work but a proviso was added to the agreement allowing those booksellers who had been accustomed to have their binding done indoors, to retain their men. The committee was then reappointed to further negotiate with the employers for the formation of articles which should give binding effect to the propositions in both Societies.

Mr Faulkner's account of the subsequent proceedings is as follows: 'In less than a month after the hour was given (that is, promised, for it did not come into operation till 29th September,) I made proposals to the masters for their consideration, for the future regulation of the trade. They were speedily adopted and were as follows: That no society man should work for an underworking master – that no master should employ a non-society man – that subsistence money should be allowed to men out of employ – that men should be struck from underworking masters upon complaint being made to me by the master appointed to transact the secret business of the trade – that men should be struck from work if refused the hour [this applied to non-society masters only] – and lastly, that the masters should pay two thirds of the expenses. These measures being agreed to gave me great satisfaction, and encouraged me to proceed in an endeavour to prevent an undue number of apprentices; for at that early period I foresaw that the bible binders would injure the trade in a few years. It was an attempt that required caution, for it was not to the interest of the trade to differ with the masters who had so recently acted honourably by us. I therefore determined to prevent this in the first instance, by checking the system away from the metropolis. For this purpose I corresponded with the trade, and sent printed circulars to every city and market town in England, Scotland, Wales, and Ireland, stating that there was a redundancy of journeymen, and that, in consequence, only four could be permitted to come to London yearly; informing them at the same time that should they not pay the necessary attention to the notice, they could not obtain employ-ment. I had the power, and in gross instances made use of it. If the men had been true, and faithfully kept their promise, I think now that in a great degree success would have attended my endeavours in an attempt to persuade the London masters to assist in putting a stop to a practice that sooner or later must be injurious to all connected with the trade.'

The foregoing propositions laid before the Masters' Society by Mr Faulkner were agreed to as nearly as possible, and formed the basis of a plan of conjoint action. One thing should be here noted: previously, no subsistence money, or out-of-work pay had ever been granted by the Lodges, support only being given to those who were called out or locked out on some trade dispute, when a levy was imposed on the members. Under this joint agreement men out of work were to receive six shillings per week, towards which the associated employers were to pay three shillings and sixpence; while those called out to enforce this agreement were to receive fifteen shillings, of which the employers were to give ten shillings. A new code of laws regulating both Societies was at once framed, and as those for the men contemplated a rigid exclusion of non-society men, a working ticket was sketched out for the purpose of distinguishing those entitled by apprenticeship to exercise the craft from others. Who was responsible for the design is not clear, but Mr Faulkner suggested the motto 'United to support but not combined to injure,' which has ever since been the motto of the societies. The plate was engraved by Mr Timbury; the size of the card was $5 \times 3\frac{1}{8}$ inches, and our illustration is a reduced facsimile.

3

Pressmen Apprenticeship Prosecution 1798

'Hail friendship! softener of the human heart';
'The happy few, who offer at thy shrine,
'Care cannot wound with half so deep a stroke,
'As meets the selfish churl, when ills surround,
'And ill will come, though virtue guard the door'.

THE pressmen were among the earliest in the industry to organise in a trade union. They were highly skilled workmen and were extremely careful about admitting to their ranks anyone who had not served his apprenticeship.

This care to protect their craft is seen in their 'consideration of a young man's credentials'.

On 21st July 1875, W. H. Cooke, who had been before the committee of the Amalgamated Association of Pressmen on several previous occasions, applied for a card, having brought further evidence and his uncle as a witness.

It was proposed and seconded that he go before a magistrate and make an affadavit that he was the eldest son of his father. An amendment that he have a card was carried by 10 to 2.

The motion suggests the principle of patrimony or, in other words, 'inherited from one's father or ancesters'. This principle of patrimony was recognised in all of the old guilds and early societies.

For instance, the Articles of the original Society of Papermakers 14 said:

> No one shall be entitled to the business unless he has served a legal apprenticeship of seven years and who can produce his lawful indenture (except the elder son of a papermaker, who is to be deemed a worthy member at the age of twenty-one, provided he is brought up to the trade) also a card of freedom, before he receives a turn and, when employed, he shall deliver up his card into the hands of the clerk of the mill's company on or before the first club night after being employed.

Thus, we find the earliest guilds, friendly societies and what are now recognised as trade unions arising among journeymen whose skill and standard of life had been for centuries encouraged and protected by legal customary regulations as to apprenticeships, and by the limitation of their numbers.

Journeymen pressmen, for example, like other skilled handicraftsmen, were steeped in guild tradition and closely associated with the compositors, as a rule men of education and almost aristocratic exclusiveness, better trained and better paid than the mass of wage earners.

Their apprenticeship regulations, their high premiums and entrance fees long maintained a virtual monopoly of their craft in the hands of skilled tradesmen, in whose ranks the masters themselves had, for the most part, served their apprenticeships.

But this protection of their craft, the early principles of patrimony and the legal standing by which these early journeymen worked their trade, this did not save them from persecution when in 1798 they attempted to secure a restriction of the number of apprentices working within the printing houses of London.

This Indenture Witnesseth that John Jacob, son of Art Jacob, Paper Maker of yᵉ Parish of Southstonham in yᵉ county of South[amp]ton hath put himselfe, and by these presents doth voluntarily and of his owne free will and accord put himself Apprentice to Henry Portall, Paper Maker of yᵉ Parish of Frifolk in yᵉ affore s[ai]d County to learne yᵉ art and mystery of Paper making, after yᵉ manner of an Apprentice to Serve him from yᵉ date hereof, for and During yᵉ Term of five Years next Ensuing During all which Term Apprentice his s[ai]d Master faithfully shall serve his Secretts, keep his lawful Commands, gladly everywhere Obey, he shall doe no Damage to his s[ai]d Master nor see it to done by Others without letting or giving notice thereof to his s[ai]d Master, he shall not Wast his Masters Goods nor lend them unlawfully to any. He shall not Commit Fornication nor Contract Matrimony within the said term; at Cards, Dice or any other unlawfull Games, he shall not play whereby his s[ai]d Master may have Damage w[i]th his own Goods, or yᵉ Goods of others. he shall not Absent himselfe, Day nor Night from his master's service without his leave; nor haunt Ale-houses Taverns or Play-houses, but in all things behave himself as a faithfull Apprentice ought to doe During yᵉ s[ai]d Term & yᵉ said Ma[ster] shall use yᵉ utmost of his endeavours to teach or cause to be taught or Instructed yᵉ said Apprentice in yᵉ Art and Mystery he now followeth, and procure and provide for him Sufficient Meat, drink, Apparle Lodging, and washing, fitting for an Apprentice, During yᵉ s[ai]d Term, and at yᵉ end of yᵉ s[ai]d Term to give him a new Suite of Cloaths, And for yᵉ trew performance of all and every yᵉ Covenants and agreement either of yᵉ s[ai]d parties bind themselves unto yᵉ other by these presents. In witness thereof they have interchangeably put their hands and Seales this Twenty Ninth day of Sept[embe]r in yᵉ Second Year of yᵉ Reigne of our Sovereign Lord George by yᵉ Grace of God of great Brittaine France & Ireland King Defender of yᵉ faith Annoq[ue] Dom. 1715.

Signed Sealed & Interchangeably
Delivered in yᵉ presence of us   Henry Portal

William Taylor
Richard Willard

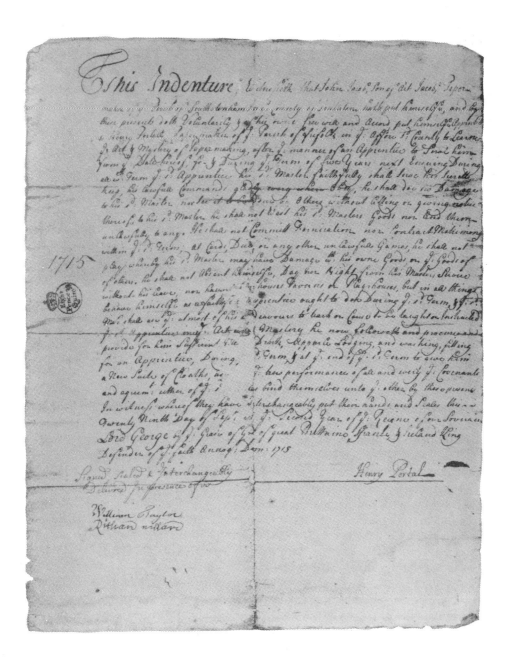

Indenture for the apprenticeship of a young man to Henry Portal, 1715.

An early steam printing machine.

It led them into a similar experience to the bookbinders in 1786, five of their number being sentenced to two years' imprisonment in Newgate Gaol for conspiracy.

In 1799 a booklet was printed titled 'An Account of the Rise and Progress of the Dispute between The Masters and Journeymen Printers', exemplified in 'The Trial at Large' with remarks thereupon and the speeches of Messrs. Knapp, Raine and Howell, both on the trial and at the time of passing sentence together with those of the Counsel for the Prosecution, with notes and illustrations upon the whole.

This booklet was published by The Journeymen Pressmen for the benefit of the men in confinement in Newgate Gaol, named Edward Atkinson, Luke Ball, John Turk, John Warwick and Nathaniel Lynham.

All of them were members of a trade Friendly Society of Pressmen, which held its meetings at The Crown, near St. Dunstan's Church, Fleet Street. The charge was an 'Indictment for a Conspiracy' on Saturday 7th July 1798 at The Old Bailey. They were sentenced three months later to two years' imprisonment.

The booklet gives an account of the case for the prosecution and the defendants' Counsel's speeches and illustrated notes where the five prisoners disputed the lies and false evidence produced by the prosecuting masters. It is a remarkable document when one considers the legal restraints then enforced by the Combination Laws of the times in which these men lived and by which they were charged. The introduction is as follows:

TO THE READER

It being customary for those who intrude themselves upon the public to apologise for so doing, we deem it necessary to say, that finding our case has excited much enquiry and concern, not only among the gentlemen of our own business, but also among many others, at once respectable and numerous, we think it our duty to caution our friends, and the public in general, against confiding in vague and erroneous report.

We are sorry to have too much reason to recommend this caution, from the strange and unaccountable explanations given by some; whilst we, on the other hand, are as happy to embrace this opportunity of returning our sincere and grateful thanks to those friends, who have so nobly stepped forward to alleviate, in some degree, the punishment inflicted upon us; to explain which it is the intention of the following pages as well as to show how far we have really merited it.

'Hail friendship! softener of the human heart';
'The happy few, who offer at thy shrine,
'Care cannot wound with half so deep a stroke,
'As meets the selfith churl, when ills surround,
'And ill will come, though virtue guard the door'.

But let the Reader always bear in mind, that the law says, however good the intention, however good the motive, it is not the subject of consideration in this case, but the deed itself! We therefore humbly submit the account of the *Rise and Progress of the Dispute*, which occasioned the prosecution; firmly declaring, that every step taken by us in the business was done with the sole view of putting an end to the continual calvil, on the score of apprentices; and what considerably excited us to this, was the happy effect a similar proceeding had been attended with a few years back.

For a considerable time, previous to the year 1794, we can safely aver there was not a week passed, but that, in some printing office or other, discussion arose concerning the price of work, scarcely two paying alike. It was suggested to the Masters, that it was essential to the peace of all concerned in the business, to have a scale of prices, that all masters might pay the same sums for similar work.

After much solicitation on the part of the men, this was complied with; and, as it produced the desired effect, we were encouraged to flatter ourselves that a similar arrangement, with respect to apprentices, might be beneficially adopted; allowing each master to take in proportion to the number of men he employed; and this measure, we trusted, would have been followed by the same pleasing consequences to both parties.

The Reader may rely upon the truth of the statement, and the remarks made thereon; as we solemnly declare we have no other motive than to explain the object we had in our minds, and to offer it as a beacon to other Societies. Not only will these members see how egregiously we were deceived in our expectations, but we hope, sincerely hope, it will also put our friends on their guard *how* they act, *however good their intention, however good their motive.*

> E. ATKINSON
> L. BALL
> J. TURK
> J. WARWICK, and
> N. LYNHAM

N.B. By means of this prosecution it has been attempted to persuade the public, that our intention was to hinder the masters from taking *any* apprentices; this we flatter ourselves does *not* appear in evidence, but that the contrary fact is made manifest.

On Saturday the 7th day of July 1798, Edward Atkinson, Luke Ball, John Turk, John Warwick and Nathaniel Lynham were tried at the Old Bailey, upon an indictment for a conspiracy, the first count of the indictment states:

First Count:
That on the 7th of April, in the 38th year of King George III, with force and arms, at the parish of St. Bridget, alias Bride, in the Ward of Farringdon, did unlawfully assemble and meet together, and being so unlawfully assembled and met together, then and there unlawfully, wickedly, and unjustly, did conspire and combine, confederate and agree together, by direct means, as much as in them lay, to restrain and prevent the said masters in the said art, mystery, and occupation from taking too many apprentices in the said art, mystery, etc., etc.

Second Count:
With force on arms unlawfully, wickedly, corruptly, and maliciously, did conspire, combine, confederate, and agree together, by indirect means, as much as they lay, to prevent and restrain the said masters in the said art, mystery, and occupation from taking so many apprentices in the said art, mystery, and occupation as by law they were entitled to do, to manifest prejudice and destruction of the said art and mystery of printing, etc., etc.

Third Count:
Wickedly, maliciously, by indirect means, as much as in them lay, to prejudice, aggrieve, impoverish, restrain, and obstruct the said masters in the said art, mystery, and occupation, in the due, fair, and lawful exercise of the great and manifest prejudice and destruction of the said art, mystery and occupation of printing, to the great injury, ruin, and impoverishment of the said masters, in the act, mystery, etc., etc.

The indictments against the five pressmen indicated that the journeymen pressmen had endeavoured, by indirect means, to prevent and restrain the masters from taking so many apprentices as by the law they were entitled to do.

This was a rather curious accusation, since the journeymen very well knew that the law entitled a master to have, as they themselves quoted, 50, 500, 5,000 or any other number, however large, if he, the master, chose to bind them. The five accused men stated during the trial.

'But the reason of a moderate man says, that too many apprentices introduced into the trade cannot fail to overturn that occupation where such undue numbers of apprentices shall be introduced, although it be according to the law, as even the apprentices themselves, so taken, when their time should expire, would find the utmost difficulty, if not utter impossibility of procuring a comfortable subsistence by that profession they had laboured seven years to obtain a right to follow.'

The further curious fact concerning this prosecution was that the masters themselves complained 20 years previously to the court of the Company of

Stationers, and that the members of that court, having similar ideas as the journeymen pressmen, passed the following resolution:

STATIONERS HALL

'At a court held on Tuesday the 7th March, 1775, complaint having been made of some masters of this company binding too many apprentices, it is ordered that for the future, every master before he binds an apprentice shall send into court, in writing, to the master, a list of the names of the apprentices he has at such time in his service, and is further ordered that the said orders shall be printed and hung up in the lobby of the court room.'

The pressmen in their defence of the indictments, stated, the above order had been copied from a table hung up in the lobby of the court room of the Company of Stationers. Since the above order it has been the constant practice of the stationers' company, to make every person who wished to bind an apprentice sign a paper, expressing how many he had; and for many years. They refused to bind more than four to any one journeyman, therefore, it was not reasonable to ask, why it had been discontinued?

Once again therefore, this prosecution of journeymen printers was not about matters concerning the trade, but the fear of the master printers and the establishment of Government, who considered it an act of treason for a combination of men to meet to discuss matters of their trade, albeit, that to regulate and advance the situation within the trade at the time was as important to the masters as well as the journeymen.

The prosecution was in the first instant pursued by one Jonas Davis whose establishment was in the area of Blackfriars, London. Three years previously he had been involved in bringing a conspiracy charge against the journeymen pressmen working in his establishment, over the same problem, employing or bonding nine apprentices to one journeyman, to which his pressmen objected.

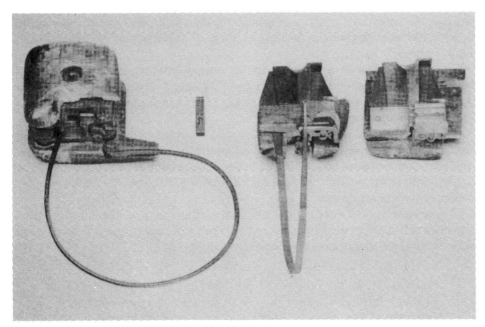

Pressmen's Tools.

This prosecution, which was held at Hicks Hall, Clerkenwell, Jonas Davis instructed his solicitor to withdraw. In the words of the time 'It was removed by a Certiorari.' It seems the main reason he withdrew the conspiracy charge was because he himself was being charged at Hicks Hall at the same time for 'assaulting' an apprentice within his employment.

It was Jonas Davis, who again was the main master within the Master Printers' Association, who instigated the dispute between the masters and pressmen in 1798 by still employing cheap bonded apprentice labour to which the journeymen companionship objected.

But this time the companionship decided to negotiate, as stated in their 'To the Reader' publication to arrive at a similar arrangement in respect of apprentices as they had done on prices three years previously.

After various letters being passed between them in February 1798, the master printers met with the five named pressmen on 10th March at the York Hotel, Bridge Street, Blackfriars, London.

The principal spokesman and leader of the pressmen was Edward Atkinson, secretary of the Pressmen's Companionship. After discussions about the number of apprentices bonded to any master, and bearing in mind the stationers' company order some 20 years previously, the pressmen put forward five main points:

1. That there should be three apprentices to seven presses, allowing another should be taken when the eldest was in the last year of his time.
2. No boy to be admitted upon poundage unless he be turned over (meaning no boy receiving the same advantage, without previously serving a regular apprenticeship).
3. No apprentice to be permitted in any house, beyond a reasonable time of trial, without being turned over (regular apprenticeship).
4. Apprentices not to be allowed equal to journeymen, nor less than what will properly support them.
5. No apprentices to be taken pending the negotiation.

Following further discussions they agreed to give the masters some time to consider the proposals, agreeing it was not in their interest or the masters in the meantime to stop the trade, or for the masters to do anything that was prejudicial to the workmen.

There then followed a further meeting at the York Hotel in April, which concluded it would assume that an agreement was reached in part, but which Jonas Davis did not or would not accept, resulting in the journeymen giving notice to a withdrawal of their services.

This withdrawal of service instigated the prosection of conspiracy by the master printers and the Crown, even though the master printers had been party to the meetings, and technically made themselves guilty of conspiracy under the law of the day by combining together to meet and discuss the very problem which the five pressmen were being charged.

Following a very detailed and complicated trial, during which the London pressmen still stuck to their principle of the number of apprentices, the recorder of London summed up and gave his judgement:

> 'I am almost perfectly satisfied, there exists a club of journeymen,
> who meet for the purpose of providing for those who are bold
> enough to offend against the law of their country, who are bold
> enough to say, work only for masters who comply with those
> regulations we have imposed.

Pressmen 1800.

'Such a club as that have they instituted to support those who may be punished. I am stating this from the facts proved, after the Secretary and Committee are proved to have conspired, one should have thought that, before three months had expired (prisoners had to wait three months in prison before being sentenced), they would have been prepared to make every acknowledgement to the country; but that not being so I am of the opinion, the conspiracy being fully proved, and the leniency of the court not having the desired effect it is my duty, to prevent such conspiracies by passing this sentence, which is, *that each of you be confined for two years in Newgate, but that your imprisonment be reckoned from the day of your commitment.*'

LET US LABOUR

Brother, exert they noblest powers,
Time will not be always ours,
Then let us labour while we may
And give to life a brighter day.
Let us work with heart and hand
To bless ourselves and bless our land,
To gather light from minds of worth,
To scatter light o'er all the earth;

Banish ignorance, give death to crime,
Write Virtue's name on passing time;
Let Freedom's banner be unfurled,
And tyranny from our earth be hurled.
Where men have dared in truth's fair light
To grapple with oppressive might,
Let us help them in the strife,
For earnest work is freedom's life.

To strike the fetters from the slave,
To honour but the truly brave,
To crush what falsehood feeds upon,
My brother let us labour on.
And though we struggle hard and long,
We yet shall sing our triumph song;
And all the Majesties of earth
Shall homage give to honest worth.

Manchester   *Joseph Hutton*
26th June, 1863

4

'Bloody Black Jack' gaols the Times Pressmen 1810

We covet not our masters' wealth,
Nor crave for nothing more
But to support our families
As our fathers have before.

THE way of the trade unionist in the eighteenth and early nineteenth centuries was rough and full of danger. The Combination Acts then in force made it an offence for workers to combine to advance wages, or reduce hours, or to affect in any way those who carried on any manufacture of trade.

Offenders might be convicted and committed to gaol for a period not exceeding three months, or sent to hard labour for two months. These Acts, although they contained clauses applicable to employers as well as employees, were in practice never applied to employers, even when they combined to depress wages.

They were in fact used solely as instruments to persecute the workers, who were instinctively combining to prevent their standard of life from being cruelly debased by the growth of industrialism.

Earlier statutes, before the Acts of 1799 and 1800, had already made combination of working men or women illegal (as was shown in the prosecution of the early London Bookbinders recorded in 1787) but Parliament did in those earlier times recognise the obligation resting upon itself and upon the Courts to regulate wages and conditions.

When this legislative protection was swept away, the Acts of 1799 and 1800, lasting until 1824, became a piece of shameless class legislation.

As an illustration of what has just been written, the observations of Francis Place, a Member of Parliament, and a 'great reformer' of the early nineteenth century, may be cited. He said concerning the prosecution in 1810 of the printers employed on *The Times:*

> 'The cruel persecutions of the Journeymen Printers employed on The Times newspaper in 1810 were carried to an almost incredible extent. The judge who tried and sentenced some of them was the Common Sergeant of London, Sir John Sylvester, commonly known by the cognomen of "Bloody Black Jack" . . . No judge took more pains than did this judge of the unfortunate printers, to make it appear that their offence was one of great enormity, to beat down and alarm the really respectable men who had fallen into his clutches and on whom he inflicted scandalously severe sentences.'

And, as so often happens when repressive measures are introduced, the Combination Act, designed to destroy the trade unions, did in fact strengthen the sense of solidarity among them.

George White, 'the energetic Clerk to the Hume Committee' (a Parliamentary Committee of Enquiry into Combinations of workmen and others matters, appointed in 1824, of which Joseph Hume, MP was chairman), said that the Act of 1800 had been 'in general a dead letter upon those artisans upon whom it was intended to have an effect – namely, the shoemakers, printers, papermakers, shipbuilders, tailors, etc, who have had their regular Societies and Houses of Call, as though no such Act was in existence.'

Although the journeymen printers, or the early combination of pressmen were among the earliest to organise in a trade union, little is known of the early years, since because of the Combination Acts, records were either not kept at all or kept in secret because of fear of prosecution.

The earliest recorded evidence shows that the London Union of Pressmen was established in 1834, but in fact present-day research (still being carried out) has established that 'Lodge Companionships' did exist in 1798, when five of the pressmen's leaders were sentenced to two years' imprisonment for 'conspiracy' in attempting to secure a restriction of the number of apprentices.

They were members of a Trade Society of Pressmen which held its meetings at 'The Crown', near St. Dunstan's Church, Fleet Street, and it was stated by the prosecution that 'by means of some wicked men among them, this Society degenerated into a most abominable meeting for the purpose of a conspiracy.'

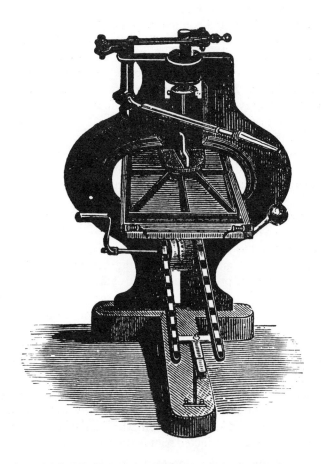

The Times *was established on 1st January, 1785, under the name of* Daily Universal Register. *On 1st January, 1788, at its 940th number, it changed its title to the* Times *or* Daily Universal Register. *The introduction of the Stanhope Press (above) in 1800 led to an average production of 150 completed copies per hour.*

Further to this we have the observations of Francis Place on the prosecution of the compositors and pressmen in 1810 who, despite the repressive legislation of the time, submitted a wage claim for an increase in the weekly wage of four shillings a week. This resulted in 21 of their number receiving fines and imprisonment in Newgate Gaol of between 9 months and two years.

From the notes of the trial at the Old Bailey on Thursday, 8th November, 1810, Stephen Hurley, Robert Howlett, Roderic Paskin, John Gee, Edward Kidd, William Clifton, Stephen Becket, Guy Warwick, Thomas Woolley, Henry Byrne, William Williams, Corbett Latham, William Cay, James McCartney, John Mackintosh, Nathaniel Collins, Malcolm Craig, John Chapman, George Westray, William Wentworth and John Simpson, pressmen and compositors on the establishment of *The Times* newspaper, were indicted for 'combining' and conspiring together maliciously to injure their masters and employers by quitting their work on account of their demands for an increase of wages not being acceded to.

A Mr Alley, prosecuting, stated the case for the prosecution, conceiving it to be a case which called for the best attention which the jury could give to it and contending that the issue which they had to try between the country and the prisoners was one which was of utmost importance to society.

He would produce a cloud of witnesses to prove to their perfect satisfaction that every person then at the bar was guilty of a combination, not only for the purpose of getting an increase of wages for themselves, but to prevent others from working at the accustomed prices, and that the gentlemen of the jury must know that *The Times* was a diurnal newspaper, and that an incalculable injury might be done to the establishment by workmen refusing to work for a single night.

He then indicated that the prisoners had made no demand for an increase of wages until some men from the office of *The Day* called upon them in May, telling them 'they hoped they would ask for an advance of wages as others had done; that they had new opportunity of retrieving their character; and if they did not do so they would be looked upon as "rats", as they always had been'. *The Day* men also told them there was an association formed into which they would be admitted if they demanded the increase.

The compositors agreed to make the demand too, and to give notice leaving their employment if it was not acceded to. This notice was accordingly given the next day, and the day after the pressmen sent a similar notice. Mr Walter, the acting proprietor, was excessively surprised at this notice as he stated he had granted them many indulgencies and had done everything that a kind master could do to make their situation comfortable.

Nevertheless, 28 of his men did actually leave him. He stated that he had often, in the course of his practice, witnessed combinations among workmen, without however any particular mischief being intended to their master.

The prosecutor then went on to say that he would show that the malice of the men was so great that, on the morning that they quitted their employment, it was proposed to 'bishop the balls' which meant to wet the balls used for blacking the types with water, so as to make them unserviceable for some time.

Mr Alley went on further to say, 'a witness of the name of Beverridge would prove to the jury that he had been invited to attend a meeting at the Coach and Horses in Water Lane, where he found a meeting which pretended to be a charitable or Friendly Society, but where in fact contributions were made to support those workmen who were out of employ in consequence of their striking for an increase of wages'.

Among the resolutions of this conclave, they had even dared to record in their books that no man should, for six months, work in the place of any person who struck on account of the increase being refused him.

At this point in the trial, Mr John Walter stated that he and his father were proprietors of *The Times* newspaper and that all the prisoners were in their employ, and it was not to him personally, or in his presence, that the men demanded the increase of wages, but after notice given to Mr Crowe and Mr Street, publishers.

The prisoners left his work upon the 28th of May. The compositors had given their notice of quitting on 12th May and the pressmen on the 14th May, the former therefore quitting him on 26th May and the latter on 28th May, Westray, Simpson and Wentworth, compositors, quitting him on 29th May.

Considerable further evidence was produced by the prosecution, not only on a conspiracy to raise wages, but a conspiracy to perpetrate murder by perjury, indicating plots to obtain the arrest of men in the dead of night from the Lord Mayor on the false charge that two men still working were deserters from the navy.

The prosecution even went for the landlords of the public houses in which the prisoners met. To quote the Common Sergeant in his summing up, which lasted one and three quarter hours: 'It appeared too that these gentlemen had private rooms in public houses, with the cognizance of the landlords, for the furtherance of their pernicious purposes; it would be for the magistrates thereafter to consider whether such landlords ought to have a renewal of their licence.'

Having given some of the background insofar as the proprietors and the Crown were concerned, just what was it that the companionships of both compositors and pressmen were asking which caused such indictments to be brought against them. It seems to be an increase in wages of four shillings per week which had already been agreed to within the printing houses of London by a Standing Committee of Master Printers.

Bearing in mind, as indicated earlier, that a combination of employers was just as illegal as a combination of workers, it was quite clearly admitted at the trial that there was a Standing Committee of Master Printers.

Applegath's Vertical Rotary Printing Machine, 1848. As metropolitan dailies continued to require faster printing machinery, engineers adopted the rotary printing principle. Men at eight 'stations' fed sheets into the machine, which printed on them from type clamped to the vertical drum at the centre.

Although Mr John Walter, on being cross-examined by Mr Gurney, the prisoners' QC, said that he admitted that in making a communication with one of the prisoners, Mr Westray, who was acting as foreman of the Companionship, Westray had behaved himself with decency and respect. He said he conceived it his duty to make the communication, he could not recollect whether he had or had not said that they might strike or leave his employment if they thought it proper, or whether he had shown Westray a letter from the Committee of Master Printers indicating an increase in wages.

But he knew that there was an agreement among the trade to give an advance of four shillings a week to the compositors of the first class, and he was therefore disposed to give half to the compositors of the duplicate. It was upon that principle that he had before offered an increase of 18 pence when he supposed that three shillings was to be the increase to the other class of pressmen.

Mr Street, the publisher of *The Times,* remembered some of the pressmen having applied through him for an increase and that upon communicating with Mr Walter, he had acceded to the increase on one part of their work, but not on other work. He further agreed that 14 days' notice (which had been given by the men) was the usual one in the trade and that the wages of the pressmen amounted to 13 shillings per week, and their hours of work were, on average, between 15 and 16 one day and between 10 and 11 the next.

Old Newgate Gateway, 1750, from an old print in the British Museum. The windmill (top) was for ventilation.

37

Trying to put all the facts together, 173 years on, bearing in mind there were indications at the trial that the increase asked for was being paid within the trade, proper notice being given before their withdrawal of labour, the summing up by the Recorder and the sentences he passed certainly indicate a cruel persecution – not I suspect for asking for an increase or for striking but because they combined together to achieve it.

At the Old Bailey on 11th December, 1810, the address and sentence were pronounced.

11th December, 1810, Old Bailey

The recorder addressed the prisoners (19 of the 21 charged on 8th November, 1810) to the effect:

'Prisoners you have been convicted of a most wicked conspiracy to injure the most vital interests of those very employers who give you bread, with intent to impede and injure them in their business and indeed, as far as in you lay, to effect their ruin. The frequency of such crimes amongst men of your class in life, and their mischievous and dangerous tendency to ruin the fortunes of those employers which in principle of gratitude and self-interest should induce you to support, demand of the law, that a severe example should be made of those persons who shall be convicted of such daring and flagitious combinations, in defiance of public justice, and in violation of social order. No symptom on contrition on your part has appeared – no abatement of the combination of which you are accomplices has yet resulted from the example of your conviction. Persons of your description must, therefore, be taught to feel the effects of that contumacy in which they presume to wrestle with the laws of the land, and to set up their daring combinations and edicts against the good order and well being of society, and the interests of honest industry in this country.'

The Judge then passed the following sentences on the prisoners respectively:

Stephen Hurley	Fined 1/- 12 months' imprisonment, Newgate.
Robert Howlett	Fined 1/- 2 years' imprisonment, Newgate.
Roderic Paskin	Fined 1/- 9 months' imprisonment, Newgate.
John Gee	Fined 1/- 2 years' imprisonment, Newgate.
Edward Kidd	Fined 1/- 9 months' imprisonment, Newgate.
William Clifton	Fined 1/- 18 months' imprisonment, Newgate.
Stephen Becket	Fined 1/- 18 months' imprisonment, Newgate.
Guy Warwick	Fined 1/- 12 months' imprisonment, Newgate.
Thomas Woolley	Fined 1/- 12 months' imprisonment, Newgate.
Henry Byrne	Fined 1/- 12 months' imprisonment, Newgate.
William Williams	Fined 1/- 9 months' imprisonment, Newgate.
Corbett Latham	Fined 1/- 9 months' imprisonment, Newgate.
William Cay	Fined 1/- 9 months' imprisonment, Newgate.
James McCartney	Fined 1/- 9 months' imprisonment, Newgate.
John Mackintosh	Fined 1/- 9 months' imprisonment, Newgate.
Nathaniel Collins	Fined 1/- 9 months' imprisonment, Newgate.
Malcolm Craig	Fined 1/- 9 months' imprisonment, Newgate.
John Chapman	Fined 1/- 9 months' imprisonment, Newgate.

Accused of conspiracy to 'ruin' the employers, 21 Times *employees were fined and imprisoned in Newgate gaol.*

George Westray	Fined 1/- 9 months' imprisonment, Newgate.
William Wentworth	Fined 1/- 9 months' imprisonment, Newgate.
John Simpson	Fined 1/- 9 months' imprisonment, Newgate.

The Printing Machine Branch of the old National Union of Printing, Bookbinding and Paperworkers (SOGAT '75, now SOGAT '82) celebrated the Pressmen's Centenary in 1934 with a dinner. The souvenir programme said the Pressmen's Union was the first real attempt to co-ordinate the activities of the Guilds or Gifts which had been in existence for many years prior to that date.

The Gifts were small groups each associated with a certain public house, such as the Punch Bowl, the Gentlemen and Porter, and the Forty Thieves. The latter, we have on the authority of the souvenir programme, 'was an exclusive society consisting of forty members at whose meetings forty pots of ale and forty "screws" of shag were religiously placed before them at the commencement of their proceedings'.

TRANSPORTATION

'From distant climes, o'er wide spread seas we come,
(Though not with much eclat or beat of drum)
True patriots all, for be it understood,
We left our country for our country's good.'

Henry Carter 1796

ON 12th May 1787 the first fleet of transportation convicts set sail on its journey from Portsmouth, England, to Botany Bay, Australia. Of the eleven ships which sailed, with instructions to find and set up a penal colony, nine were chartered from the East India Company, three being used as store ships, six being convict ships carrying seven hundred and fifty-nine convicts. The convict ships were named The Alexander, Lady Penrhy, Charlotte, Scarborough, Friendship and the Prince of Wales. To accompany this fleet of convict ships there were only two naval ships, H.M.S. Sirius and Supply. Their duty was to escort and defend the fleet both at sea and upon their arrival at Botany Bay. Thus began the transportation over the next seventy years of 158,702 male and female prisoners.

The route, or ports of call of the first fleet, were Santa Cruz Roads, Teneriffe, Cape Frio, Rio de Janeiro, Table Bay in the Cape, passing Van Diemans Land, better known today as Tasmania, not wishing to land due to bad weather and the possibility of hostile natives. This journey took them over eight months. Bearing in mind that at the beginning of the journey Government records say:

> 'The prisoners were thoroughly washed and issued with new clothing before being embarked, but occasionally were put aboard in a filthy state. The regulation dress for the men comprised jackets and waistcoats of blue cloth or kersey, duck trousers, check or coarse linen shirts, yarn stockings and woollen caps. These clothes were suitable for a summer voyage, but were altogether too light for winter. The naval authorities objected on hygienic grounds, however, to flannel and woollen garments, contending that these materials harboured disease. In consequence, the lightly-clad convicts, whose bed-clothing was limited to a single blanket, suffered acutely from cold in the winter months and in the high southern latitudes. In the prison hulks whilst waiting transportation they wore woollen clothing and the substitution of lighter clothing when they were sent to the convict ship in cold weather often led to sickness.'

The convicts on arrival must have been suffering from all kinds of contagious or infectious diseases or in such a debilitated condition that their chances of surviving the rigours of the long voyage were slight.

However, the first ship to arrive was H.M.S. Supply, which arrived at Botany Bay on Friday 18th January, 1788, the rest of the fleet on Sunday 20th January, 1788. They landed at Solander which had been found and named by Captain Cook but Botany Bay was found not to be suitable to start a settlement as it was all marshland and the harbour was too shallow. Within a few days expeditions had been sent out and they finally came across Port Jackson which was more suitable. Eventually the convicts were allowed on dry land and the first penal colony in Australia was started.

Political Poster W. Crane.

41

Death of an Old Radical

IF the 'Trade Circulars' of the old Bookbinders Consolidated Union did not exist today, the obituary entitled 'Death of an Old Radical' which was contained within a circular of the 26th December, 1872 would not have led to the following story.

OBITUARY

Our obituary of to-day contains a notice of the demise, in the Royal Infirmary, of a man named Andrew White, who took a prominent part in the agitation for Parliamentary Reform in 1819–20. Deceased was 72 years of age, a native of Glasgow, and was employed as a bookbinder. He was present at the memorable gathering at Bonnymuir on 5th April, 1820 and was, along with Andrew Hardie, John Baird, and a number of others, apprehended on a charge of high treason. The prisoners were tried by a special commission at Stirling in the month of July, same year, and Hardie and Bairdwere, as is well known, sentenced to death, and were executed on September the 8th. A capital sentence was also passed on Andrew White, but a petition having been forwarded to the Home Office in his behalf, his sentence was subsequently commuted to transportation for life. He was afterwards, along with a number of others, sent to Botany Bay, which was then a penal colony. After remaining some time there an English gentleman succeeded in engaging him as a servant, and brought him to this country. On leaving the service of this gentleman, White came to Glasgow and resumed his trade as a bookbinder. He was a widower, and has left no relations, as far as is known. The body of deceased will to-morrow be interred, by his own request, besides the remains of Hardie and Baird, in Sighthill burying ground. It is said that White was the last survivor of the men who suffered punishment in connection with the Bonnymuir affair; and the consent of the managers of the burying-ground, to his interment in the place he desired, was obtained by an old confrère, Mr. James Mitchell, painter, King-street.

5

Andrew White – Bookbinder

Example sheds a genial ray
Of light which men are apt to borrow,
So first improve ourselves to-day
And then improve our friends tomorrow.

THIS is the tragic story of a young Glasgow bookbinder, Andrew White, and a band of Scottish workers who were caught up in the struggles during the early part of the eighteenth century for political democracy.

This was a time when to act on the basis of one man one vote as the birth right of any man was considered by the ruling class to be voicing treason against the State. To write or to demonstrate for political reform was considered by the State to be revolutionary and, therefore, to be an act of High Treason. To be convicted of High Treason during this part of the eighteenth century still carried that barbarous punishment of being hung, drawn and quartered. A remittance of this sentence, by the Grace of the King and State, was to be hung and the head cut from the body, with private burial being allowed. To be extremely lucky meant transportation to the Colonies.

These then are the turbulent times in which Andrew White, Bookbinder, was to become one of the many Scottish Radical Martyrs.

To do justice to the story of Andrew White and the other Scottish Radicals, it is necessary to outline the background of the political times leading up to that gathering at Bonnymuir in April of 1820.

The Government was a Government of the property owning class – indeed in his journals 1831–1854 Lord Cockburn, Whig Leader, wrote:

> 'So long as property, upon which our whole system has long been founded, shall continue to return the House of Commons, I shall not despair, but if the elective qualification shall be reduced so low that the property element is made merely nominal and a greatly increased proportion of that House shall be returned by mere population, I fear that our boasted constitution must soon sink into that democracy which seems to be the natural result of every Government where the people have become politically free.'

His, and many others of his class's thinking at that time was, of course, that only the due influence of the property class could maintain a stable country. To them, to give one vote to all would immediately bring about a revolution, and their greatest fear was a French type of revolution developing in the United Kingdom.

Spies and Agent Provocateurs

This then led the Government, or at any rate the active members of it, namely Lords Sidmouth and Castlereagh, to engage and appoint spies and agent provocateurs, whose instructions were to go about among the leaders of militant sections of the workers, to encourage them in treasonable oaths and acts, and generally provide victims for the scaffold. (Any needing evidence of this only need to visit the Public Records Office at Kew or in Edinburgh, where this information has been kept under the Secrecy Acts for nearly a century.)

It was, of course, no concern of their Lordships that innocent workers would be lured to transportation, or destruction, and that their wives would be made homeless, widows and their children fatherless.

Their concern was class policy, statecraft, and the convincing of the property owning middle classes that the flames of another 'French Revolution' was ever ready to burst forth, and for that reason all property interests ought to renounce any electoral reform and they should support the power of the landed gentry.

Diligently these Agent Provocateurs in Scotland organised the hungry workers (mainly weavers), and urged them to take treasonable oaths, and sedulously they spread false information that a great rising was being planned in London and that the King's hated Ministers were to be murdered and indicating that soon a signal would come for a rally. At the same time, they transmitted to the authorities the name of every honest leader and rebel spirit who heeded their lies.

The Call to Arms

And then, when all was ready for the 'Radical Rising', treasonable placards were posted by Government Agents, and the duped workers rushed to their doom. How astonished the middle class citizens of the West of Scotland must have been on Sunday, the second day of April, 1820, as they went on their way to church and saw staring at them from every hoarding and gable end a call to arms which had been posted during the night by Government Agents.

This, and more, was for forty miles around Glasgow simultaneously exposed, even on church doors. In Glasgow great crowds stood on the streets all day, with hovering expectation on their faces. Various accounts are to be had of the scenes which followed, the Whig writers minimising and the Tory writers exaggerating the 'crisis'. The Radicals confined their narrative to Glasgow.

A modern day picture of Stirling Castle, where the Bonnymuir prisoners were held, from 5th April 1820 till their transportation to the prison hulk 'Bellerophon', lying off Sheerness.

ADDRESS

TO THE

Inhabitants of Great Britain & Ireland:

FRIENDS AND COUNTRYMEN,

ROUSED from that torpid state in which We have been sunk for so many years, We are at length compelled, from the extremity of our sufferings, and the contempt heaped upon our Petitions for redress, to assert our RIGHTS, at the hazard of our lives; and proclaim to the world the real motives, which (if not misrepresented by designing men, would have United all ranks), have reduced us to take up ARMS for the redress of our *Common Grievances.*

The numerous Public Meetings held throughout the Country, has demonstrated to you that the interests of all Classes are the same. That the protection of the Life and Property of the *Rich Man*, is the interest of the *Poor Man*, and in return, it is the interest of the Rich, to protect the poor from the iron grasp of DESPOTISM; for, when its victims are exhausted in the lower circles, there is no assurance but that its ravages will be continued in the upper: For once set in motion, it will continue to move till a succession of Victims fall.

Our principles are few, and founded on the basis of our CONSTITUTION which were purchased with the Dearest Blood of our ANCESTORS and which we swear to transmit to posterity unsullied, or PERISH in the Attempt. – Equality of Rights (not of Property,) is the object for which we contend; and which we consider as the only security for our LIBERTIES and LIVES.

Let us show to the world that We are not that Lawless, Sanguinary Rabble, which our Oppressors would persuade the higher circles we are – but a Brave and Generous PEOPLE, determined to be FREE, LIBERTY or DEATH is our *Motto*, and We have sworn to return home in *triumph* – or return *no more!*

SOLDIERS.

Shall YOU, Countrymen, bound by the sacred obligation of an Oath, to defend your Country and your King from enemies, whether foreign or domestic, plunge your Bayonets into the bosoms of Fathers and Brothers, and at once sacrifice at the *Shrine of Military Despotism*, to the unrelenting Orders of a Cruel Faction, those feelings which you hold in common with the rest of mankind? Soldiers. Turn your eyes towards SPAIN, and there behold the happy effects resulting from the Union of Soldiers and Citizens. Look at that quarter, and there behold the yoke of hated Despotism, broke by the Unanimous wish of the People and the Soldiery, happily accomplished without Bloodshed. And, shall You, who taught those Soldiers to fight the battles of Liberty, refuse to fight those of your own Country? Forbid it Heaven! Come, forward then at once, and Free your Country and your King, from the power of those that have held them *too, too* long in thraldom.

Friends and Countrymen. The eventful period has now arrived, where the services of all will be required, for the forwarding of an object so universally wished, and so absolutely necessary. Come forward then and assist those who have begun in the completion of so arduous a task, and support the laudable efforts, which we are about to make, to replace to BRITONS, those rights consecrated to them, by MAGNA CHARTA, and the BILL of RIGHTS, and Sweep from our Shores, that Corruption which has degraded us below the dignity of Man.

Owing to the misrepresentations which have gone abroad with regard to our intentions, we think it indispensably necessary to DECLARE inviolable, all Public and Private Property. And, We hereby call upon all Justices of the Peace, and all others to suppress PILLAGE and PLUNDER, of every description; and to endeavor to secure those Guilty of such offences, that they may receive that Punishment, which such violation of Justice demand.

In the present state of affairs, and during the continuation of so momentous a struggle, we earnestly request of all to desist from their Labour, from and after this day, the First of April; and attend wholly to the recovery of their Rights, and consider it as the duty of every man not to recommence until he is in possession of of those Rights which distinguishes the FREEMAN from the SLAVE; viz; That, of giving consent to the laws by which he is to be governed. We, therefore, recommend to the Proprietors of Public Works, and all others, to Stop the one, and Shut up the other, until order is restored, as we will be accountable for no damages which may be sustained; and which after this Public Intimation, they can have no claim to.

And We hereby give notice to all those who shall be found carrying arms against those who intend to regenerate their Country, and restore its INHABITANTS to their Native Dignity; We shall consider them as TRAITORS to their Country, and Enemies to their King, and treat them as such.

By order of the Committee of Organization,
GLASGOW, 1st April, 1820   for forming a Provisional Government.

Britons. — God. — Justice. — The wishes of all good Men are with us. — Join together and make it one Cause, and the Nations of the Earth shall hail the day, when the Standard of LIBERTY shall be raised on its *Native Soil.*

THE PROCLAMATION OF THE 1820 RISING

The lull before the storm

In this turmoil we should follow the register of events as they affected Andrew White during this class war uprising, when workers openly and boldly declared to their Masters that they would work no more until the Government of the country was changed. The situation was turning into a large-scale, though spy-fomented, strike for political freedom – a strike which the bulk of the participants expected would end in a bloody but successful revolution.

The news from England gave no indication that London had been captured; and the Government troops in Scotland were being swiftly moved to points of vantage, awaiting the Radical Coup D'Etat. Local eruptions were disregarded; the Government was in no hurry, the troops could bide their time until a radical army of ill-armed, ill-disciplined rebel workers had gathered, and then in one great carnage would be taught a lesson that would serve to humiliate two or three generations of discontented common folk.

The March to Bonnymuir

Meanwhile, in our story the Government spies were active, and on Wednesday morning, 5th April, 1820 they succeeded in inducing a party of about eighty Glasgow men, Andrew White amongst them, to march upon the Carron Iron Works at Falkirk, where it was said an army from the English Provisional Government (Revolutionary Government) would shortly arrive, and assist the Glasgow men in seizing the Government cannon there.

Eighty ill-armed men, some of them Lord Castlereagh's spies, marched via Condorrat and Castlecary. Among the marchers was Andrew Hardie, a young weaver and ex-army sergeant. At Condorrat they were joined by John Baird, the village smithy, but by this time, with one excuse after another, the spies melted away and finally the expedition was reduced to fifty in number who arrived at Bonnymuir straight into the arms of the 10th Hussars. The troops dashed upon them, the marchers crouched behind a dyke and fought desperately until almost every one of them was wounded, many being killed. The fight finally ending with the nineteen weary and wounded men that night being prisoners of war in Stirling Castle. This then was the end of the great Battle of Bonnymuir.

The Aftermath

In Glasgow for a time the wildest stories were rife. French vessels had landed arms and money on the Ayrshire coast, the English Rebel Army had grown to 80,000 men, the Carron Iron Works had been captured, and Government Troops defeated; but the truth soon leaked out and when the treachery of the spies who had urged the march upon Falkirk became known – none durst trust his neighbour. The wildest rebels were most suspect, and in this depression and suspicion the 'Revolution' fell to pieces in a single night.

Many marched in those days to lay all night in the cold and wet waiting, their spirit broken and knowing that they had been duped and were now marked men, and they wisely scattered for home. In other areas blood was shed, for in many towns the military fired upon the mobs. A riot took place in Greenock where the jail was stormed and despite magistrates, military and volunteers, five radical prisoners were set free, leaving six men killed and twelve wounded in the struggle.

BATTLE OF BONNYMUIR

An Account of the Battle which took place at Bonnymuir, on Wednesday the 5th April, 1820, betwixt about 50 of the Radicals and a party of the Military; with the names of the 15 Radical prisoners. — Also, the names of those Killed and Wounded at Greenock, on Saturday the 8th.

KILSYTH, 5th APRIL 1820.

This morning a gentleman residing in this parish belonging to the Falkirk troop of Yeomanry Cavalry; left home to join his troop at Falkirk, and had proceeded a short way from his own house, when he came up with between 25 to 30 Radicals, all armed with pikes, muskets, and pistols, who stopped him and requested him to give up his arms, which he refused to do, and showed them a disposition to resist. They told him (at the same time presenting at him several pistols) that resistance would be vain, as they would kill him on the spot. He, however, got off retaining his arms and meeting with an Orderly from Kilsyth going with dispatches to Stirling, informed him it would be improper to proceed. They accordingly both returned to Kilsyth and reported, when the Commanding Officer there ordered ten men and a serjeant from the 10th Hussars and as many of the Yeomanry Cavalry, to escort the Orderly and the other Gentleman on their several roads, and to endeavour to fall in with these armed Radicals if possible. The Radicals, in the interval, had been joined by a number more, who proceeded along the Canal Bank towards Bonnymuir, having taken several fowling-pieces and a pitch-fork from farmhouses in the neighbourhood of Bonnybridge.

The Cavalry, on their arrival at Loanhead, being informed of their proceedings, immediately went to Bonnymuir in search of the Radicals, and, on coming up with them, they showed a disposition to fight rather than fly; having taken their position behind an old dyke, they allowed the Cavalry to come within thirty yards of them, when they fired a volley; the Cavalry instantly charged, firing a few shots when going over the dyke; the Radicals received the charge with their pikes, and made all the resistance in their power, but they soon found themselves in a bad situation, and throwing away their arms, endeavoured to escape, when the Cavalry secured nineteen prisoners; three of whom are wounded, two remained on the field so badly wounded as not to be able to be carried to Stirling Castle, where the prisoners are lodged. Eight or ten of those who escaped are said to be wounded, and have not been able to go from the place where the affair happened. The whole number of the Radicals did not exceed forty or fifty. None of the Cavalry are severly wounded; two are slightly in the hand; and one horse severely wounded in three different places (since dead) and a number of horses slightly.

It is reported that the whole of the prisoners belong to Glasgow, except one of the name of Baird, said to be their leader, who lately resided at Condorrat. It is said that the whole had been drilling in the Calton Green of Glasgow this morning, that they left that place about four o'clock, and went over the country in a straggling way till they arrived at Bonnymuir, where they expected to be joined by a number from all parts of the country during this evening and tomorrow.

NAMES OF THE PRISONERS.

John Baird,	Andrew Hardie,
Thomas McCulloch,	John Barr,
William Smith,	Benjamin Moir,
Allan Murchy,	Alexander Latimer,
Alexander Johnston,	Andrew White,
David Thomson,	James Wright,
Thomas Pink,	Robert Gray.
James Cleland,	

Saturday morning, about three o'clock, the prisoners were put on board a Steam Boat at Stirling, under the charge of a Macer of Justiciary, and a party of the 4th Veterans. They were landed at Newhaven, where six carriages were waiting for them to be conveyed to the Jail.

Names of the Killed and Wounded at Greenock.

Names.	Age.	Wounds	
Adam Clephane,	48	Under the groin.	Dead.
Archibald Drummond,	20	Shot dead through the Chest	Dead.
James Kerr,	17	Through the belly.	Dead.
John McWhinnie,	65	Through shoulder and chest.	Dead.
Hugh Paterson,	14	Through the leg.	Leg amputated.
John Patrick,	30	Through the thigh.	Doing well.
David McBride,	14	Through the cheek and jaw.	Doing well.
A. McKinnon,	17	Through chest and arm.	Doubtful.
Catherine Turner,	65	Through the leg.	Leg amputated.
		The above in the Infirmary	
John Boyce,	33	Through the belly.	Dead.
George Tillery,	25	Through the thigh.	Doing well.
Robert Spence,	11	Slightly in the foot.	Slightly.
William Lindsay,	15	Shot dead on the spot.	Dead.
James McGilp,	8	Ball in right thigh.	
Gilbert McArthur,	18	Through the left thigh.	Flesh wound.
John Turner,	22	Through the calf of the leg.	Flesh wound.
Peter Cameron,	14	Through the right leg.	Flesh wound.
John Gunn,	24	Through calf of left leg.	

Printed for John Muir.

Meanwhile, the middle classes had rallied to the aristocracy. A bag of radical reformers had been secured and the Lords of Government wanted a 'Lesson on the Scaffold'. But worst of all, the workers as a class had ceased to believe in themselves; the trail of treachery and spying led everywhere and anyone's next door neighbour might be in police pay.

A Lesson on the Scaffold

The surviving Bonnymuir marchers were tried for High Treason. John Baird and Andrew Hardie were sentenced to be hung, drawn and quartered – this sentence and barbarous proceedings being carried out and specially intended to impress the workers. The others, including Andrew White, were sentenced to transportation for life.

The sentence on Hardie and Baird was carried out on September 8th, 1820. Before leaving Stirling Castle for the scaffold, Hardie and Baird were granted permission to pay farewell to those taken prisoner with them and after these addresses were finished they individually embraced each other and took a most affectionate farewell. White and another boy, Johnson, were particularly affected and clung to Hardie until they were ordered away to their cells.

On the 11th October, 1820, a month after the execution of Hardie and Baird, the remaining 19 prisoners were received from Edinburgh on board the hulk 'Bellerophon' lying at Sheerness to await transportation, the sentence of Andrew White now remitted to 14 years transportation.

The hulk 'Bellerophon' was none other than the famous Royal Navy Ship HMS Bellerophon on which, following his defeat at Waterloo, Napoleon Bonaparte was received by her Commander, Captain Frederick Maitland, at Rochefort on 15th July, 1815.

From the log of the ship 'Speke' carrying 156 convicts to New South Wales, Andrew White was No. 149 on the list. The ship sailed during December, 1820, arriving four months later in New South Wales.

A drawing of the time, showing the hulks at Sheerness.

Speke
156 Male Convicts
Sailed December 1820

Name	Where Convicted	When	Term
Robert Gray			Life
John Anderson			to be indented to
Andrew Dawson			the contractor
Allan Murchie	Stirling Oyer and Terminer	25 August 1820	for 7 years
Thomas McFarlane			
John McMillan			
James Clelland			
Benjamin Muir		5 September 1820	
Alexander Johnstone			14 years
David Thomson			to be indented
William Clackson alias Clarkson	Stirling Oyer and Terminer	25 August 1820	to the contractor for 7 years
Alexander Hart			
William Smith			
Thomas McCulloch			
Alexander Lattimer			14 years
Andrew White	Stirling Oyer and Terminer	25 August 1820	to be indented
James Wright			to the contractor
Thomas Pike alias Pink			for 7 years
John Barr			

Copy of Log of the ship 'Speke'. Sailed 13th December 1820 with 156 male convicts aboard for New South Wales arrived May 1821.

A transport ship carrying convicts

New South Wales – Activity and Intrigue

There is little doubt that one-hundred and sixty years ago, Andrew White would have been considered the luckiest of the nineteen Scottish Radicals who arrived in the ship 'Speke' and that he would have been envied by not only the other eighteen, but by all the other convicts and ticket of leave men who could not get home for, although he had been sentenced to fourteen years in New South Wales, he left the colony to return to the United Kingdom less than three years after his arrival, having been granted an absolute pardon by the Presiding Governor, Governor Brisbane, in 1824.

The story behind this began partly before, and not long after, Andrew White began his first assignment as a House Servant along with Alexander Hart another Scottish Radical, to Dr. Douglass a local magistrate and Superintendent of the female factory.

Generally the lot of a House Servant would be considered dull and uninteresting but Andrew White could not have so regarded it for the house of Dr. Douglass seems to have been the subject of activity and intrigue. This is certainly confirmed by reading notes on colonial papers and despatches from Governor Brisbane to Lord Bathurst in respect of Dr. Douglass and activities in the colony available at the Records Office, Kew. The reason for this activity and intrigue and Dr. Douglass not being popular with some of the exclusive settlers was mainly because of his concept of promoting the welfare of convicts not being acceptable to them. There were three in particular, who were also magistrates, Samuel Marsden, Hannibal Macarther and Sir John Jamison, as it was their desire to maintain a supply of cheap convict labour, and it certainly appears from the historical records that they and others seem to have had a conspiracy to ruin the reputation of Dr. Douglass and drive him from public life.

Governor Brisbane, who by all accounts had similar views to those of Dr. Douglass, and who aimed at the re-habilitation of convicts rather than use them as slave labour or a source of cheap labour, stood behind the Doctor when matters reached a showdown in the case of a female convict called Ann Rumsby, described by the Governer in his despatch of 6th September, 1822 as a 'young and handsome convict girl', who had unwittingly become, together with Andrew White, a pawn in the politics of the colony.

Love and Marriage

A situation arose where Dr. Douglass had taken Ann Rumsby from the female factory, where he was the Factory Superintendent, on a temporary basis to supplement his house staff which resulted, after a period of time, in young Andrew White confessing to the Doctor that he had fallen in love with her and asking for permission for them to marry. However, the Doctor in his wisdom withheld his permission, indicating that this was because of Andrew White's youth – he was only eighteen at this time whilst Ann Rumsby was twenty. Also, during this time Dr. Douglass had been asked, and given his consent, to a William Bragge a convict servant at Parramatta Hospital to marry Ann and the Rev. Samuel Marsden had proclaimed the banns for the marriage on 4th August, 1822.

The Conspiracy

Ann Rumsby was in a dilemma because she did not wish to marry William Bragge. She, unfortunately, confided her problem to a Dr. James Hall who had visited the Douglass home and who already knew Ann Rumsby having been the ship's surgeon on the 'Mary Ann' which had brought her to New South Wales to serve her seven year sentence.

He posed as a friend and she, not knowing that Doctor Hall was deeply involved with Samuel Marsden one of the magistrates in opposition to Dr. Douglass' reformist views, told him that Dr. Douglass would be her ruin, meaning she had no wish to marry William Bragge because she did not like him.

This she explained to Andrew White when he questioned her about what had passed between her and Dr. James Hall. Dr. Hall in an affidavit afterwards twisted what she had said to infer that Dr. Douglass had taken liberties with her and he wrote a letter about this to Samuel Marsden, who with four of his fellow magistrates, refused to sit on the same bench with Dr. Douglass.

They then summoned Ann Rumsby before them and subjected her to an hour-long period of questioning on oath, hoping she would produce her incriminating evidence against her master, Dr. Douglass, but to her credit she remained firm stating that he was a good employer and master and had taken no liberties with her. As a result of this the five magistrates accused her of perjury.

Governor Brisbane, believing Ann Rumsby was telling the truth, wrote in a despatch to Lord Bathhurst:

> '. . . had I displaced Dr. Douglass I would have countenanced the sentence of the magistrates condemning for perjury *a female unprotected prisoner,* to whom they had promised indemnity in case she spoke the truth; yet because she spoke not the truth, as they would have it spoken, condemned her to banishment for the remainder of her sentence.'
>
> The magistrates, by banishing Ann Rumsby for the remainder of her sentence intended to send her to the penal settlement at Port Macquarie, which by all accounts was a 'hell hole'.

The intrigue and conspiracy had now come to a head and the Governor removed the five individuals from the magistracy, for he realised that the whole six magistrates, which included Dr. Douglass, could not remain in the same commission and act in the same neighbourhood, without them becoming violators instead of conservators of the peace, and as he recorded in a further despatch to Lord Bathhurst in his opinion Dr. Douglass' single service to his, (The Governor's) Administration had 'redounded to the honour of His Majesty's Government more than the united efforts of any of the five magistrates in the territory.'

Disappointment and Free Pardon

The final outcome of this game of intrigue to the pawns involved, was that Ann Rumsby still had to marry William Bragge, like it or not. This took place on 3rd February, 1823 and our radical colleague was compensated for his lost love by the gaining, on the 17th February, 1824, an absolute pardon which enabled him to accompany Dr. Douglass to England a few days later. Governor Brisbane had commissioned the Doctor to return to England to consult with the Colonial Office in London on the function of a new Court of Requests he had set up and to which he had nominated Dr. Douglass as Commissioner.

Day Book

Governor Sir Thomas Brisbane 1824

19 Feb.   Lt. Gov. Erskine's salary for performing the Duties of Lt. Gov. during the last twelve months.

21 Feb   Dr. Douglass's appointment as

Commiss. of the Court of Requests. A new court established by virtue of the New South Wales Indicative Act. Salary be fixed at £300 per ann.

Dr. Douglass journey to England on the affairs of the Colony. His passage should be paid by the public.

23 Feb   Mr. T. Cudberts Grant of Land

Andrew White sailed with his master in the ship 'Ocean' on the 25th February 1824, a week before the granting of pardon was promulgated by being published in the *Sydney Gazette* on 4th March, 1824. In 1825 the general muster of all inhabitants in the colony includes, with Andrew White's details, the statement 'Went to England with Dr. Douglass'.

The story has been full of incident and intrigue but fact is stranger than fiction. Unfortunately from the time that Andrew White returned to England nothing more is known until his death, this being reported in the Bookbinders Consolidated Union Minutes of 26th December, 1872.

However, mystery still remains. His Death Certificate describes him as seventy-one years of age, but as he was supposedly born in 1804, the date recorded on his King's Pardon and the only date so far discovered, he would have been only sixty-eight or sixty-nine at the time of his death in 1872. The year 1804 is probably correct, but in that event he would have been only sixteen years of age when captured, a mere boy. This to a degree is supported by the information concerning the parting with Hardie at Stirling Castle, indicating that the two youngest prisoners, White and Johnson, being the most affected, and also, of course, Dr. Douglass' subsequent objection to the marriage.

Monument to Hardie and Baird, Sighthill burying ground, Glasgow.

As pointed out in the obituary, his last wish was to be buried with his radical comrades. This wish was carried out and has since been confirmed, but by all accounts, the latter part of his life seems to have been fairly lonely.

THE FIRST FOUR VERSES OF
THE SORROWFUL LAMENTATIONS OF
THOMAS BLIZZARD AND JOHN SARNEY

Who were Sentenced to Die, at the late Commission for the County of Bucks, held at Aylesbury, on the 10th of January, 1831, they being the leaders of the Rioters and Machine Breakers in and near High Wycombe, Bucks.

You must the feeling heart deplore,
This sad and awful time,
When want misleads the Labouring Poor,
To misery and to crime;
And now upon the fatal drop,
To meet the public eye,
Two poor men in a healthful state,
Must a sad example die.

Thomas Blizzard, is one of these men,
His age is thirty years,
He has a tender loving wife,
And three small children dear;
John Sarney is the other man,
His age is fifty-four,
He has six children and a wife,
His case for to deplore.

To see their loving wives and friends,
Come to see these wretched men,
Such a horrid sight, I hope that we,
May never, never see again;
I hope this will a warning be,
To all and every one,
And never throw yourselves away,
By visiting unlawful bands.

In Aylesbury dark Condemned Cell,
These wretched men do lay,
Awaiting for the mournful knell,
To Summons them both away;
May God in mercy take their souls,
By penitence made pure,
And yet with comfort cheer the hearts
Of the industrious Poor.

6

Wycombe 'Swing' Paper Riots 1829

Rags make Paper,
Paper makes Money,
Money makes Banks,
Banks make Loans,
Loans make Beggars,
Beggars make Rags

The nineteenth century opened with all papermakers talking and speculating on the advent of a machine which would make an endless web of paper – the employers wondering whether the prospects would justify the capital outlay needed, the journeymen papermakers anxiously considering the effect this machine would have on their livelihood.

By March 1816 the journeymen papermakers of 'The Original Society of Papermakers' in Maidstone presented a petition to the House of Commons stating that 'they were reduced to the greatest distress by dimission from factories due to the introduction of endless paper machinery, which requires few hands to work it and those of little experience and praying that machinery should be suppressed.' There were further petitions on the subject in the next two years, but nothing came of them.

By the end of the Napoleonic Wars, unemployment and destitution had produced outbreaks of violence in all districts of the country and these were fanned by the general call for political reform and by March 1817 the Habeus Corpus Act was suspended by the Government and stringent acts and penalties were passed against sedition.

Although through the 'Eighteen-Twenties' our journeymen papermakers, along with workers from other trades, anxiously watched these machines upsetting their livelihood and the poverty they brought with them, the most distressed were the farm labourers because of the introduction of the threshing machine, which they considered took away their winter employment, thus increasing the tension, hunger and disturbances. These disturbances became known as the 'Swing Riots'. The first threshing machine was destroyed at Lower Hardres, near Canterbury in East Kent, on the night of 28th August, 1830. The precise date is worth recording for two reasons, one as the breaking of machines was to become the characteristic feature of the Labours' Movement of 1830, which started in Kent, spread over a score of counties in the next three months, and secondly confirms that the riots known in the Wye Valley as 'The Wycombe Paper Riots' were in reality part of the Agricultural Labours 'Swing Riots' which swept through twenty counties of England between August 1830 and went on until the last recorded episode in the whole 'Swing' movement which was the destruction of a threshing machine at Tadlow in Cambridgeshire in September 1832.

Machine breaking, whilst the most significant, was only one of the numerous forms that the Agricultural Labours' Movement assumed. Arson, threatening (or 'Swing') letters, wages meetings, attacks on justices and overseers, riotous assemblies to extract money or provisions, or to enforce a reduction in rents or tithes – or even of taxes – all played their part and can be divided into five distinct phases; first fires reaching into all neighbouring counties of Kent and Surrey; secondly the wrecking of threshing machines; thirdly late in October 1830 wages meetings accompanied by

radical agitation against taxes and rents; fourthly wages meetings and machine breaking, and finally in early November further rounds of fires, threatening letters, riots and machine breaking. But in the end, the reaper had his reward for during these fourteen months of unco-ordinated actions, special court commissions were set up which resulted in 1,976 prisoners being tried by 90 courts sitting in 34 counties, tabulating the sum total of their sentences as follows:

Sentenced to Death	252
(of these 233 commuted, mainly to transportation)	
Executed	19
Transported	505
Prison	644
Fined	7
Whipped	1
Acquitted or bound over	800

These sentences followed the usual pattern of the times. There were, as indicated, 19 executions, but all but three of them were for arson, yet in terms of men transported they were quite remarkably severe. No less than 481 persons of the 505 stated were wrested from their families and shipped 12,000 miles away with virtually no hope of ever returning to their homes, resulting in the South of England with whole communities being stricken for a generation by the blow.

But our story is about 137 people, 46 papermakers and a number of farm labourers caught up in this 'Swing' movement within the Wye Valley of Wycombe on and for some days after 29th November, 1830. At the beginning of November of that year, the Duke of Buckingham, Lord Lieutenant of Buckinghamshire, issued a circular to the magistrates which was in accordance with instructions he had received from the Secretary of State, Lord Melbourne. These instructions were to be issued to all associations of Trade Guilds within towns and areas, indicating that they were to be held responsible for defending property against riots. To assist in this they were empowered to enrol night-watchmen and special constables.

The instructions required returns from the magistrates of the county to show what necessary precautionary action had been taken, although by all accounts up until the time of receiving these instructions very few disturbances seem to have occurred within the county. It is all the more surprising, therefore, that by Friday, the 26th November, 1830, a committee of twelve was appointed at the Guildhall of High Wycombe to aid the civil power. This committee comprised of a representative from the Church, Law and Industry of the General Area and, of course, therefore included several owners of paper mills within the Wye Valley.

This may have been prompted by the fact that in the second week in November there were reports of 'Swing' letters at Colnbrook and Langley and at Marlow, and High Wycombe farmers and papermakers began to be beseiged with letters threatening to destroy their crops and buildings, or machines if these were not removed. One such letter, dated 11th November, 1830, ran:

This is to acquaint you that if your threshing machines are not destroyed by you directly, we shall commence our labours.

Signed on behalf of the whole
'SWING'

Some farmers took the hint and began to dismantle their machines and, in some paper mills, the erection of new machinery was suspended. But even with these warnings and anticipations, the form that the initial outbreak took must have come as somewhat of a surprise, for the attack, when it came, was directed only marginally

Assemble to the sound of a horn on Flackwell Heath.

57

against threshing machines and farmers, and almost exclusively against the machinery installed in half-a-dozen paper mills along the three-mile stretch between Loudwater and West (then Chipping) Wycombe.

On the 24th November came the first specific warning of trouble in that the paper workers themselves, 300 of whom were said to be unemployed, indicate they would march on the mills and destroy the machinery. Two days later, on market day, a great meeting of paper workers took place on Rye, half-a-mile out of High Wycombe, to protest against the continued use of machinery; and from there 'an immense multitude' (to quote *The Times*) marched into the town, invaded the hall where the justices and householders were assembled, and turned their meetings into bedlam.

The Riot Act was read to no avail and the presiding magistrate was even persuaded to send the Buckinghamshire Yeomanry Cavalry away in order to appease the crowd. Some rioters collected hammers and began to march on Messrs Lane Mill with the intention of destroying the machinery forthwith. The attempt, however, failed and the operation was postponed until another day.

On the 29th November from 5 o'clock in the morning, paper workers and labourers began to assemble to the sound of a horn on Flackwell Heath. Indications locally are that secret meetings were held previously at the 'Leathern Bottel' on Flackwell Heath and a plot hatched to dismantle the paper machines, the Innkeeper being one John Sarney, aged fifty-four.

He along with another papermaker, Thomas Blizzard, a much younger man, being the Ringleaders; both later to be condemned to be hanged.

Flackwell Heath is some four miles east of High Wycombe. Many of the papermakers and labourers who answered the horn that morning were armed with sledge-hammers, sticks and crowbars. The local justices also arrived and again read out the Riot Act, but feelings were running high and the justices were overwhelmed and the High Sheriff was wounded by a stone thrown by one of the crowd.

The rioters then marched on to High Wycombe through Wooburn Green and Loudwater, picking up supporters on the way, and at 9 o'clock made their first stop at John and Joseph Lane's paper mill on the outskirts of West Wycombe. The 'indictment' of Thomas Blizzard and William Russell charged on 2nd December, 1830, with Felony, indicates in its opening remarks, 'A mob of persons assembled in a riotous and tumultuous manner at the paper mill of John and Joseph Lane in the Parish of Chipping Wycombe in the said county, arrived with crowbars, hammers, hatchets, axes and other terrific and offensive weapons with which they forcibly opened the said mill, etc. etc.' Two shots were fired and four gallons of vitriol acid were hurled at the rioters; but they soon broke in and destroyed the machinery, whilst the vitriol thrower was ducked in a pond. After this they went on to Loudwater, destroying a Zachary Alnutt's machinery at Marsh Green and a Mr John Hay's machinery a mile beyond. Next to Hay's Mill stood Lansdale Farm and there a threshing machine was smashed.

The rioters now halted for refreshment at the Red Lion Inn before going on to Loudwater, a mile beyond, where they completed their work by breaking the paper machines at Richard Plaistow and Robert Davis's mills.

But by now the forces of law and order had been thoroughly alerted; the Buckinghamshire Yeomanry arrived at the scene, supported by a party of red-coated huntsmen, mainly composed of local gentry, who joined in the affray. The rioters themselves by this time were suffering from exhaustion and indeed many were worse off for drink. On that day, and many following, 137 papermakers and farm labourers were arrested and charged with various offences between 29th November, 1830 and 11th January, 1831, the indictment of Blizzard and Russell, two charged with being among the Ringleaders stated as follows:

Bucks } The Information of Richard Hailey
to wit } High Constable of the second Division
of the Hundred Desborough in the
county of Bucks, taken upon Oath
this Second day of December in the
year of Our Lord, One Thousand
Eight Hundred and Thirty at and
in the Borough of Chipping Wycombe
in the county of Bucks, before us
the undersigned two of His Majesty's
Justices of the Peace in and for
the said county Bucks, on the
Examination, and in the Presence
and Hearing of Thomas Blizzard
and William Russell brought before
us, and charged with Felony, the
said Richard Hailey on Oath
says as follows:-

Between the hours of nine and ten in the morning of
Monday the twenty ninth day of November last, a mob of
persons assembled in a riotous and tumultuous manner
at the Paper Mill of Joseph and John Land in the parish
of Chipping Wycombe in the said County, armed with
Crow Bars, Hammers, Hatchets, Axes, and other terrific
and offensive weapons, with which they forcibly opened
and entered the said Mill and with great violence
broke and destroyed part of the said Mill and the
machine for making paper therein, after which the mob
which had very largely increased in numbers to the
amount of four hundred or more, proceeded through the
town of High Wycombe in a body to the Mill of Zachary
Allnutt at Marsh Green in the said parish of
Chipping Wycombe, about half a mile from the town,
Which they surrounded and instantaneously proceeded to
break open and forcibly enter with their bars and
other instruments, and demolish the Paper Machine
therein, among the most active and voilent of whom, I
saw the prisoners Thomas Blizzard and William Russell.

the former with an Iron Bar, and the latter with a
Hammer, and after the rioters finished their work of
destruction they proceeded in a similar manner to the
Paper Mill in the occupation of John Hay at the Marsh
in the said parish of Chipping Wycombe about a mile
from the Mill of Mr Allnutt, whose machine had been
partly taken down, the door of which the mob, with bars
and other instruments forcibly broke open and entered,
at the head of whom, and one of the most active and
determined was the prisoner Blizzard, and in the Mill
they destroyed the remaining part of the machine. The
armed party or most of them proceeded to the barn at
the farm of Mr Richard Lansdale opposite, and there
destroyed his thrashing machine, (part of which he had
previously taken down) in the destruction of which
also the prisoner Blizzard was actively and prominently
engaged. The armed mob which had alarmingly increased
in number proceeded to the Paper Mill of Richard
Plaistowe, at Loudwater in said parish of Chipping
Wycombe, where they met with resistance for a short
time and appearing determined to enter in. The Mill
was opened and the mob entered and immediately
set about destroying the machine which they completed,
actively assisted along by the prisoner Blizzard who
appeared to be the leader, giving the word of command
and heading the rioters. After destroying this machine
the mob proceeded to the Mill of Mr William Robert
Davis in the said parish of Chipping Wycombe about
a quarter of a mile off and there were captured
with increased assistance, which had arrived to oust
which had all the day been wonderfully overpowered
in numbers, several of the rioters. The Riot Act
was read by Reverend Frederick Vincent, Clerk one
of His Majesty's Justices of the Peace for the said
county, while the rioters were at Mr Allnutts Mill
but notwithstanding that, they determined to continue
assembled, and to go on destroying the machines.

Richard Hailey

Sworn before Geo. Scobells T. Peers Williams.

Handmade paper turn of 18th Century, forming, laying and putting the sheets to press.

Within the Calendar of Prisoners held at the gaol at Aylesbury for Felonies and Misdemeanours, the names of 46 people appear, charged with paper machine breaking, fourteen are shown below:

A CALENDAR OF THE PRISONERS
IN HIS MAJESTY'S GAOL at AYLESBURY
for FELONIES & MISDEMEANOURS

Who have taken their Trials at the Session of Oyer and Terminer and Special Gaol Delivery, holden at AYLESBURY, on Monday the Tenth Day of January, 1831, before The Honourable SIR JAMES ALLAN PARK, Knight, one of the Judges of His Majesty's Court of Common Pleas; The Honourable SIR WILLIAM BOLLAND, Knight, one of the Barons of His Majesty's Court of Exechequer; and The Honourable SIR JOHN PATTERSON, Knight one of the Judges of His Majesty's Court of King's Bench.

RICHARD WILLIAM HOWARD HOWARD VYSE,
ESQUIRE, SHERIFF

17. John Reynolds, aged 29,
18. John Walker, aged 37,
19. Joseph Priest, aged 36,
20. James Barton, aged 28,
21. Robert Cary, alias John Dell, aged 23,
22. Alfred Salter, aged 19,
23. Thomas Fisher, aged 26,

24. Richard Weedon, aged 41,
25. John Sawney, aged 54,
26. John East, aged 21,
27. William Nibbs, aged 21,
28. James Stretton, aged 19,
29. Edmund Barton, aged 24,
30. James Stone, aged 29.

Committed 29th November, 1830 by John Augustus Sullivan Esq. and the Rev. William Mussage Bradford, charged on the oaths of William Lacey and others with having on the 29th November last, unlawfully, riotously, and tumultuously assembled together, to the disturbance of the public peace, at the mill and in the premises of Mr William Robert Davis, at the Parish of Chipping Wycombe, in the said County, and feloniously were present, aiding, abetting and assisting divers persons, to us as yet unknown, with the feloniously and unlawfully destroying certain machinery used in the manufacture of paper in the said mill, used in carrying on the trade or manufacture of a papermaker, at the mill and on the premises of the said William Robert Davis, at the Parish of Chipping Wycombe aforesaid, in the County of Bucks. aforesaid, against the form of the statute in that case made.

Reynolds, Priest, James Barton, Salter, Fisher, Weedon, East, Nibbs and Edmund Barton – Judgement of Death Recorded; Walker and Stretton – No True Bill, Discharged; Cary, alias Dell – No Prosecution, Discharged; Sawney – Guilty, Death; Stone – Acquitted.

Out of the total number of papermakers charged – Judgement of 'Guilty', Death, Two; Judgement of Death, Forty-Two; Two acquitted, one of whom was James Stone aged 29 whose defence recorded at the Special Assizes in Aylesbury was that he was 'On the Tramp' travelling from Dartford to Leicester to take up a good job, this was confirmed by the local innkeeper. As was the custom of the day, Journeymen Papermakers walked from job to job and the man on the 'Tramp' used inns with which 'The Original Society of Papermakers' had special arrangements, paid by local papermaking members, of a free night's lodging and at departure 1s. 6d. for a pint of porter and 6d. for his pocket. James Stone's story was confirmed by a Dannual Griffen, Landlord of the inn concerned, resulting in his acquittal.

Prison Hulks.

Following the judgements passed on them, the prisoners sentenced at the Special Commission held at Aylesbury on the 10th January, 1831, were committed to the prison hulks at Portsmouth, forty-six of them being papermakers, all of whom were found guilty of breaking machinery, twenty-nine of this number having had the sentence of death or the Judgement of Death passed on them, and were committed to be held on the prison hulk 'York', there to await the outcome of a Review of Sentence by Lord Melbourne, the Home Secretary, petitions being submitted on their behalf by their families and friends.

Names of those held on the hulk 'York'

Stephen Atkins	Alfred Salter
Henry Walker	Thomas Bowles
John East	Thomas Fisher
Edmund Wingrove	David Barton
William Butler	John Butler
James Barton	John Smith
Moses Holt	John Crutch
William Nibbs	Thomas Blizzard
John Sawney	Richard Weedon
John Walduck	James Miles
John Moody	Joseph Briant
William Hancock	John Dandridge
Joseph Priest	Samuel Sommerfield

Prison conditions aboard the hulks cannot be described as very comfortable, the diet of the common people in the 19th century was never very good, even amongst free men; aboard the hulks the diet and overcrowding often led to outbreaks of disease, the men were often verminous and were periodically subjected to outbreaks of the itch, typhus and dysentery.

At Woolwich in the 19th century alone, there were outbreaks of dysentery (1816), smallpox (1818), typhus (1821), inflammation of the lungs (1826), severe sickness (1827), cholera (1832) and erysipelas (1846).

All this meant the quality of life was very bad, especially when one considers the poor diet that was allocated to the prisoners, which consisted of: half-bad meat, weak soup, bread and biscuits on two days a week – known to the convicts as Burgoo Days. On the other four days oatmeal and cheese replaced the meat, and for drinking there was Thames water and a quart of small beer, if they got it; because there were frequent discrepancies in the regulations and the reality of the prison system of the day.

Whilst the men suffered these conditions, and almost as soon as their trials were over, a campaign for mercy began. Petitions were sent to the Home Office and were signed by Bankers, Church Ministers, and even the very Magistrates who had had them arrested.

The campaign had its effect as by the end of January, and the beginning of February, 1831, most of the prisoners convicted on the 10th January had received remission of sentence, if it could be called that in the case of the death sentence which had been passed on Thomas Blizzard and John Sawney – this was commuted to one of transportation for life. The other twenty-seven who had Judgement of Death passed on them were commuted to transportation for seven years.

The following is a copy of a 'Pardon' issued on behalf of Thomas Blizzard and John Sawney, one of many of the twenty-nine Prisoners Pardons in our possession – Blizzard and Sawney being the only two sentenced to be hung:

Thomas Blizzard and
John Sawney

Pardon

William R.

Whereas Thomas Blizzard and John Sawney
were at the special Gaol Delivery holden at Aylesbury
for the County of Buckingham on the 10th day of
January instant, Tried and Convicted of viciously,
wilfully, feloniously, and with force, destroying
machinery, fixed and prepared for the manufacture
of paper, and had sentance of death passed upon
them for the same. - We in consideration of some
circumstances, humbly represented unto us, are
graciously pleased to extend our Grace, and Mercy
unto them, and to grant them our Pardon for their
said crime, on condition of their being transported
to New South Wales, or Van Diemans Land, or some
one, or other of the Islands adjacent, for, and
during the term of their respective natural lives.
Our will, and pleasure therefore is that you do
give the necessary directions accordingly, and for
so doing this shall be your Warrant. ——

Given at our Court at St James, the 29th day of
January 1831, in the first year of our Reign.

By His Majesty's Command.

Melbourne.

To our Trusty and Welbeloved
Our Justices of the Special Gaol
Delivery for the County of Buckinghamshire.
The High Sheriff of the said County and
all others, whom it may concern.

WYCOMBE PAPER RIOTERS

	Court Judgement	Pardon	Boat
John Reynolds	J.O.D.	12 months' hard labour in house of correction	
Joseph Priest	J.O.D.	7 years' transportation	Proteus
James Barton	J.O.D.	7 years' transportation	Proteus
Alfred Salter	J.O.D.	7 years' transportation	Proteus
Thomas Fisher	J.O.D.	7 years' transportation	Proteus
Richard Weedon	J.O.D.	Life transportation	Proteus
John Sawney	G.D.	Life transportation	
John East	J.O.D.	7 years' transportation	Proteus
William Nibbs	J.O.D.	7 years' transportation	Proteus
Edmund Barton	J.O.D.	18 months' hard labour in house of correction	
William Beiant	J.O.D.	7 years' transportation	Proteus
William Smith	J.O.D.	12 months' hard labour in house of correction	
Henry Stratford	J.O.D.	12 months' hard labour in house of correction	
William Butler	J.O.D.	7 years' transportation	Proteus
John Moody	J.O.D.	7 years' transportation	Proteus
William Hancock	J.O.D.	7 years' transportation	
William Moody	J.O.D.	12 months' hard labour in house of correction	
Moses Holt	J.O.D.	7 years' transportation	Proteus
John Butler	J.O.D.	7 years' transportation	Proteus
William Shrimpton	J.O.D.	12 months' hard labour in house of correction	
John Dafter	J.O.D.	12 months' hard labour in house of correction	
Robert Carey	J.O.D.	7 years' transportation	Proteus
Stephen Atkins	J.O.D.	7 years' transportation	Proteus
John Walduck	J.O.D.	7 years' transportation	Proteus
Samuel Sommerfield	J.O.D.	7 years' transportation	Proteus
John Crutch	J.O.D.	7 years' transportation	Proteus
William Walker	J.O.D.	12 months' hard labour in house of correction	
John Dandridge	J.O.D.	7 years' transportation	Proteus
Thomas Blizzard	G.D.	Life transportation	Proteus
William Russell	J.O.D.	12 months' hard labour in house of correction	
John Smith alias John Budd	J.O.D.	7 years' transportation	Proteus
James Hall	J.O.D.	12 months' hard labour in house of correction	
James Webb	J.O.D.	12 months' hard labour in house of correction	
Benjamin Frances	J.O.D.	12 months' hard labour in house of correction	
John Watto	J.O.D.	12 months' hard labour in house of correction	
Arthur Wright	J.O.D.	12 months' hard labour in house of correction	
Henry Walker	J.O.D.	7 years' transportation	Proteus
David Lumon	J.O.D.	18 months' hard labour in house of correction	
David Barton	J.O.D.	7 years' transportation	Proteus
William Briant	J.O.D.	7 years' transportation	Proteus
Thomas Bowles	J.O.D.	7 years' transportation	Proteus
Edmund Wingrove	J.O.D.	7 years' transportation	Proteus
James Miles	J.O.D.	7 years' transportation	Proteus
Joseph Briant	J.O.D.	7 years' transportation	Proteus

J.O.D. = Judgement of Death
G.D. = Guilty – Death

Of the 112 convicts on board the ship 'Proteus' which sailed for Hobart Town, Van Diemans Land on the 12th April, 1831, 29 were from those convicted at Aylesbury Assizes on the 10th January of paper machine breaking, along with 3 convicted at the same Assizes for destroying a threshing machine.

The voyage took a total of four months and arrived at Hobart Town Harbour, Van Diemans Land on the 4th August, 1831.

All but one were assigned and from the Muster (Census) at the Home Office Records, Kew, by 31st December, 1835, 9 had received a 'Ticket of Leave' having served 4 years of their 7 year sentence.

The man not assigned being John Moody, aged 26, who was (report in Governor's notes) accidentally killed on service at New Norfolk. His was one of the few cases where the cause of death of any of the 'Swing' convicts was recorded. The Governor, Colonel Arthur, had his own views on the matter. He wrote to a Lord Goderich in 1837 that several of the men who had arrived in the ship 'Eliza' died immediately from disease induced apparently by 'despair'; and he indicated that 'a great many of them died due, he believed, to the despair and deep sense of shame and degradation.

A campaign to secure an amnesty for the prisoners began whilst they still lay in the prison hulks. Henry Hunt elected member for Preston, moved in the House of Commons for 'A General Pardon and Amnesty to those unfortunate agricultural and other labourers who had been tried and convicted at the late Special Commissions'; but after long debate he found only one other member of the House supporting him – a Joseph Hume. Over the next three years, however, opinions changed and, in June of 1834, Governor Arthur was directed to release one of the 'Swing' prisoners named John Boyes from Hampshire, who received a Free Pardon. A year later, in August 1835, Lord John Russell, who had succeeded Lord Melbourne at the Home Office, announced that 264 machine breakers were to be pardoned, they included 236 men who had been sent to Van Diemans Land (Tasmania) aboard the ships 'Proteus' and 'Eliza', (therefore included our 29) – that is all those sent to the island for seven years, except ten who were serving current sentences. The following year a second batch of Pardons, taking effect on 1st January, 1837, were given, which included the rest of the 'Swing' movement prisoners on a seven year term, several on fourteen, and a number of 'Lifers'. The rest were given conditional pardons by October of 1837.

In the meantime, in Van Diemans Land, bureaucracy had been at work, and 42 men, most of them from the 'Proteus' which included nearly all the Buckinghamshire men, were only released in stages and then only after energetic intercession by the Governor.

How many actually used their freedom to leave the colony, or return home to England, has so far not been established. To return home was a costly business as

ASSIGNMENTS

Name	Time	Ship	1832	1833	1835	Pardons issued 1836
Stephen Atkins	7 yrs	Proteus	John Sinclair	John Sinclair	Ticket of leave	Free or condition
James Barton	7 yrs	Proteus	Mr Davidson	Mr Davidson	Ticket of leave	
David Barton	7 yrs	Proteus	Mrs Wade	Mrs Wade	Ticket of leave	
William Beiant	7 yrs	Proteus	James Atkins	James Atkins	Ticket of leave	Free or condition
Thomas Blizzard	Life	Proteus	David Reynolds	David Reynolds	Mr McRowe	
Thomas Bowles	7 yrs	Proteus	J. Cassidy	J. Cassidy	J. Cassidy	Free or condition
William Briant	7 yrs	Proteus	James Birmey	James Birmey	Ticket of leave	Free or condition
Joseph Briant	7 yrs	Proteus	D. Lame	Hospital	Mr Seanmouth	
John Butler	7 yrs	Proteus	B. Home	B. Home	B. Home	Free or condition-
William Butler	7 yrs	Proteus	Public Works	Public Works	Public Works	Free or condition
John Crutch	7 yrs	Proteus	Lieut. Davis	Lieut. Davis	Murray Smith	Free or condition
John Dandridge	7 yrs	Proteus	Rev. P. Connelly	Rev. P. Connelly	Rev. P. Connelly	Free or condition
John East	7 yrs	Proteus	Lieut. Davis	Mr Loavis	Ticket of leave	Free or condition
Thomas Fisher	7 yrs	Proteus	J. Thomson	James Simpson	Public Works	
Moses Holt	7 yrs	Proteus	Mr Pelland	Public Works	Public Works	
William Nibbs	7 yrs	Proteus	Jospeh Home	Public Works	Public Works	Free or condition
James Miles	7 yrs	Proteus	W. Rayner	Mr Crocker	Transported to Port Arthur	
John Moody	7 yrs					
Joseph Priest	7 yrs	Proteus	John Clark	John Clark	Ticket of leave	Free or condition
Alfred Salter	7 yrs	Proteus	Mr Swan	Mr Swan	Ticket of leave	Free or condition
John Smith	7 yrs	Proteus	Mr Cawthorn	Mr Cawthorn	Ticket of leave	Free or condition
Samuel Sommerfield	Life	Proteus	Hospital	Mr Culder	Dr Dermer	Free or condition
Richard Wegdon	7 yrs	Proteus	Rev. Mc ?	Public Works	G. Kemp	
John Walduck	7 yrs	Proteus	Lieut. Hill	Lieut. Hill	Lieut. Hill	Free or condition
Henry Walker	7 yrs	Proteus	Mjr. Roberton	Mjr. Roberton	Ticket of leave	Free or condition
Edmund Wingrove	7 yrs	Proteus	Mr Story	Mr Hardy	Ticket of leave	

Compiled by Principal Super of Convict Office, Hóbart Town.
V.D.L.:
31 Dec 1832; 31 Dec 1833; 31 Dec 1835.

free passages were not provided and as far as the Governor was concerned he indicated that 'very few' could afford or wished to return to England. Another report indicated that of all the machine breaking convicts of the 'Swing' Movement who received pardons, only five or six ever returned home to England.

Secretary of State, Lord Melbourne.

Political Poster W. Crane.

7

Strangers, Travellers and Tramps 1853

He who works and does his best
Goes down the road with all the rest.

TRADE guilds arose in ways which are still obscure because most left no documents behind before the 14th century. But by then, society was in three mutual respecting and dependent parts or 'estates' – knighthood, church, and the working rest – the third estate, the working rest, embracing all from peasant and craftsmen to merchants.

When, in 1388, the Crown obliged all trade guilds to set down their rules and other information, it emerged that the network of organisation, even in those days, among the working rest was widespread, people having banded together for mutual security against poverty and misfortune because of demands made on them by the local overlord of manor or monastery.

Indeed, 'cradle to grave' seems a poor description of the trade guild services. They provided payments for apprenticeships and dowries, and carefully worked out rules for decent behaviour at annual gatherings.

These rules began with praise of the virtues of society and co-operation within the system, which have echoed down the years, providing in their way the present preamble and rules to many 18th and 19th century friendly and trade societies.

The old alliance within the crafts and in towns has been reshaped time and time again over the centuries – guilds, livery companies, craft corporations, and all their mysteries and fraternal offerings – but the basic changes came by the confrontations in the 17th, 18th and certainly the 19th centuries, as these bodies fought over wages, apprentice rules, and above all apprentice ratios and payment for the unemployed.

The richer masters speculating on unlimited profits to come from unlimited markets, provided the labour was also unlimited, found the old craft structures a hindrance and their craft philosophy an embarrassment and, in the light of the new economic wisdom, quite irrational; whereas the primary impulse of the main body of craft workers was not to change, but rather to conserve, to hold on to something slipping from their grasp.

Under these pressures, small masters and journeymen stood together, meeting within organisations described as journeymen's clubs – none more so than the early bookbinders or papermaker journeymen or their masters. Both sides turned to the law, at first with mixed results and later almost invariably to the advantage of the employers – save where the outrage was so great that legal statute was the price of social peace.

The skilled workers, much as they appealed to the law, believed that their chief strength lay in controlled entry to the trade, regulated by workshop custom and practice and apprentice ratios (these mainly running in families).

For centuries, by tradition, the weakest spot in the locally-based workshop had been the 'stranger', the 'foreigner', who when trade was bad in his own town moved on to the next or settled in the sprawling suburbs of the capital. At this stage the old custom and rules for reception of the travelling 'stranger', 'foreigner' craftsman, evolved over centuries and observed by all, embodied work, hospitality and help on the way, provided the traveller observed the rules, behaved decently at the house of

Journeyman presenting his credentials.

call and paid his bills when leaving. Usually the 'traveller' announced himself by sign, password, handshake, and later by certificate or apprentice lines.

During the 18th century, the word 'traveller' had begun to replace the word 'stranger' in trade society rules, but during the 19th century the more common usage was 'travelling brethren', 'tramping brother' or 'tramp'. There was nothing derogatory in the use of the word 'tramp', it simply meant that the member in question was 'on tramp' looking for work – today it might be an unknown brother journeyman arriving to look for work, tired, dusty, hungry and thirsty; tomorrow it might be 'you' setting out.

At the beginning, and certainly by the mid 30s and 40s of the 19th century, craft workers became more mobile as roads improved. Each year brought more strangers along the road, toolbag on back, indentures in pocket, and by tradition and custom as much entitled to work, if such there was, as the man of the town.

The itinerary of a 'Papermaker on the Tramp' is interesting. The route was prescribed, and a list of places in the order in which a journeyman should call for his turns from Maidstone.

Days Stages	Places	Miles	Days Stages	Places	Miles
1	To Chafford	23	1	To: Over Darwen	10
1	Sundridge	11	2	Milnthorp	49
1	Carshalton	18	1	Kendal	8
1	Catshall	23	1	Kirkswold	34
1	Horton	24	1	Hexham	34
1	Arbourfield	20	1	Shotley	14
1	Newbury	23	1	Newcastle	14
1	Clatford	17	1	Hilton	15
1	Salisbury	17	1	Durham	12
2	Wells	44	1	Richmond	30
2	Bradninch	50	2	Poole	45
1	Exeter	10	1	Hunslett	12
3	Cheddar	60	1	Woodlesford	5
1	Bath	26	1	Ecclesfield	26
1	Hampton	27	1	Sheffield	6
1	Winchcombe	24	1	Little Eaton	33
1	Redditch	27	3	Northampton	64
1	Birmingham	14	2	Wycombe	52
1	Kidderminster	17	1	Watford	17
3	Hope Mill	66	1	London	20
1	Affonwen	15	1	Dartford	14
3	Bugsworth	68	1	Maidstone	18
1	Charlestown	8	1	Springfield	..
1	Manchester	12	1	Turkey	..
1	Smedley	4	1	Bovil	..
1	Bury	10			

There are eleven hundred and ninety miles in the Round. The number of days for walking this distance is sixty-four, and there will be ten Sundays to rest:– making the time for absence of a journeyman ten weeks and four days, and at the end of this time from the day of the date hereof this certificate will expire, but the Secretary will then renew it if he shall be required to do so by the journeyman to whom it was granted.

It does not seem possible to say much in favour of tramping. Degrading it may have been, indeed all the evidence indicates that it was. But a glance at the tramping itinerary we have given will be sufficient to convince the reader that it was a hard life on which the tramp set out.

Some of the stages required him to walk more than 30 miles in a day. In the earlier years the man had to walk every day, through rain or snow, including Sunday, and thus had little opportunity even to keep himself properly clean.

71

As time went by, however, a little more humanity entered into the system. If a mill were near on a day of rain the mill clerk was given the power to grant another turn. And then Sunday was made a rest day. On arriving at a place on Saturday a journeyman received pay for two turns in the evening, except 8d. for the two nights' bed, and his card and book were given to him again on Monday morning.

Among the printers (outside London) where tramps were paid a penny a mile, the figure for 1863 is 180 miles a member, dwindling to nine miles a member in 1898. Out of work pay introduced in 1873 built up slowly from 10d. per member per year to 8/6d. (old money) in 1898. During 1879 tramping printers covered (or were paid for), 336,000 miles, 14 times around the world and three times the 1873 figure, despite the growing use of home donation.

'TRAMPS POEM'

For it was fifteen pence for a working day
Eighteen for the day between
And a penny for three miles over 12
When Victoria was Queen
And that was six for a bed and two for a pint
And four for a 'Rough Stuff' meal
And three for an ounce of twist of shag
To smoke when our innards did squeal

During the 1830s and early 1840s, unemployment struck when industry was plunged into two periods of depression. The effect, on top of the new pressures in a new industrial age of steam-engine capacity of British industry, was tremendous. Certainly as far as the printing trade was concerned, the periods of depression were 1836–1843 and 1846–1847.

Since no agency, other than the trade societies themselves, cared about the number of jobless workers, there were hundreds of men wandering about the country searching for work and there was little rhyme or reason about this travelling.

Fending off the hazards of journeymen 'Tramping'.

Men heard rumours of work somewhere else and set off to find it and, at the same time, men were travelling in the opposite direction, probably passing one another on the road.

The early minutes of the bookbinding societies certainly indicate that the 'travelling brothers' knew this, the trade societies knew it, but the system demanded that for full benefit they should 'walk fairly through the branches'.

While trade was fair or simply 'poor' the unemployed tramp might often be the younger man, recently out of his apprenticeship, but as the workless grew it bit into the hard-core of the society members, the highly skilled long-serving men. The Manchester bookbinders and printers saw the tramps treble in numbers during this period and record 'many diseases arise from sleeping in damp beds'. The following obituary, although recorded in the Bookbinders minutes of 24th March, 1853, is typical of the handwritten minutes recorded during the earlier years.

OBITUARY

Died on the 22nd of March, after a long and very severe illness, JOHN BREWER, aged 24 years. He joined the Manchester Society in 1849. He was a native of that town, and served his apprenticeship there. In 1852, through being out of employment, he drew his document, and after a six weeks tramp he returned with a broken constitution, brought on by exposure to the weather, and no doubt materially assisted by the bad accommodation and the usual vicissitudes that all tramps are more or less exposed to. The writer of this notice has it from undoubted authority, that up to the time of his going on the road, he never had a day's illness, and since his return he has scarcely ever been free from sickness, being a melancholy example of the effects of a system that it is quite time was done away with, and which only requires a few more cases of this kind to illustrate its effects, and it will then fall to somebody's lot to write the death of the tramping system, instead of a death from tramping.

D.B.W.

Bad as was the plight of the tramp, that of his family was far worse, for they had nothing to live on unless a man could send home part of his tramp benefit. Further extracts of minutes state: 'After three months wearisome toil he finds his family in worse circumstances than when he commenced.'

A man may avoid the workhouse whilst on the tramp but not so the family left behind; on top of which he may find on his return that he is arrested by the parish authorities and destined to the treadmill for 'neglect of family'.

Although those lucky enough to have work felt a deep sympathy for those on the roads, and the early rules of assistance and help were still carried out, with the depressions becoming more severe the tensions grew between large and small town societies, and between the North and London, and other areas outside.

Manchester spoke of hordes descending on its print and bindery shops from outside, and the London men claimed that during strikes, northern men flooded into the capital and worked there.

But slowly, as the years went by, and recurring mass unemployment, more road travel, better communication through the state of trade circulars and reports, more and more members were convinced it was becoming pointless to set off to the next town in hope of work. Better to sweat it out in the hard times at home with the family than on the road.

This, along with the consolidation of locally-based trade societies, slowly transformed the travelling brothers from heroes to villains, from an asset to a nuisance, diminishing in numbers and respect. Tramping did, however, become more and more an occupation of the union law-breakers and this, together with the discomfort and even squalor in which they lived, meant that 'working the circuit', once a point of honour, became a term of discredit and came to express itself in distaste for the members who would put up with such conditions. From this situation it was one step to equating the 'traveller' with the 'professional tramp'.

On the back of the second report of the Bookbinders Consolidated Union, is a blacklist of men throughout the country who had refused to observe the rules, headed by a representation of a 'Rat'. The list concluded with these notes:

> '*There is an execrable villain going about the country committing enormous depredations; his name is Whitlow, he is a native of Manchester, but never belonged to any Society; he is round-faced, has a glide in his eye, and an impediment in his speech. Should he make application to, or be heard by any of our Secretaries, they will please to give him in custody to the police, and send immediate word to our Secretary at Sheffield, where he has lately committed a most audacious robbery.*
> '*There is also another scoundrel just committed to Knutsford Gaol for robbing his employer; he was a horrid black sheep; and in short there is no guarantee for a man's honesty, when he refused to subscribe honourably towards the support of his trade.*'

Union members as well as their leaders were uncomfortably aware that they had 'professionals' among their own ranks and angrily aware that imposters from outside could exploit the system they had built up to care for their own members. The system was as open to abuse as any system of welfare has always been and the perennial problem of sorting out the guilty while not humiliating and penalising the innocent was more and more a matter of controversy.

Those who wanted to discard the system made the distinction between guilty and innocent less frequently. At the same time, deciding who was what became a source of friction between national and local officials, the one upholding the funds and the rules, the other having to deal with the human being, however unpopular, however suspicious.

The tramp was going down with the system and his offences multiplied with the rules designed to curb them. Tramps were accused of strike-breaking, working foul in shops banned by the union because of bad conditions, of theft, abuse, violence, indecency, fraud and embezzlement of various kinds, but above all with using the system to avoid work rather than find it, with 'chasing the sixpences' or 'working the ticket'.

The whole system of 'tramp' relief had come into discredit, and as a system of assistance for travelling brothers was abolished at the beginning of the 1850s by both the Bookbinders and Journeymen Papermakers, but revived off and on over the years until the turn of the century, unfortunately without the sympathy and hospitality of the previous centuries.

THE
SUMMER MONTHS

The Summer months are pleasant months
To those who love to roam,
And hear the forest warblers
That cheer the peasant's home;
Where nature in her brightest shades
Of light and colour glows,
And kisses with a zephyr breeze,
The honest sunburnt brows.

The Summer months are pleasant months
When bends the golden grain,
Beneath the cool refreshing winds
That sweep across the plain;
When the light of day is fading,
When labour's at an end,
And the evening songs of thankfulness
From cottage homes ascend.

When gratefully and hopefully,
Our spirits seem to rise,
And mingle with those higher forms
Whose home is in the skies;
When the clouds of night are gathering,
When the sun has left the West,
The Summer months are pleasant months
To spirits seeking rest.

Manchester   *Joseph Hutton*
26th June, 1862

Political Poster W. Crane.

8

Champions of the Poor 1880

I would not wish thee wealth, my friend,
I would not wish thee fame,
I'd wish thee something better far,
Than an empty, sounding name; –
A love for all that's truly good
And worthy of esteem,
A noble life, with thoughts as pure
And sweet as an angel's dream.

FREDERICK Rogers and Robert Banner, both members of the Bookbinders' Companionship, played important parts in the early struggles of the Labour movement.

When Rogers died members who had known him during his working life felt he should have been buried in Westminster Abbey.

Robert Banner was also a considerable worker for the Labour Party and a confirmed socialist. He was one of the first election agents for the Labour Party and acted as agent for Keir Hardie, the first Labour MP ever to be elected.

A self-educated bookbinder with a love of literature and a moral fervour to right the wrongs of 19th century industrial society, Frederick Rogers was a great speaker, writer and pamphleteer. He became president of the Vellum Binders and first chairman of the Labour Party and was born on 27th April, 1846, the eldest of five children. His father had been a sailor who eventually became a dock labourer. His mother, Susan, when she was only 17, had walked from the village of her birth to London, a distance of 40 miles.

This was because there were no prospects at all of finding work in the village, and the alternative was the dreaded workhouse. From this environment Rogers inherited his non-conformist religious fervour which was material in casting the die that shaped the future for us all.

The historian E. P. Thomson, in his excellent book 'The Making of the Working Class', shows all too plainly the debt the working class has to religion.

Unintentionally, the churches and chapels taught our forefathers how to organise and administer beyond the running of their own day-to-day affairs – from being poorly educated, in a world where one had to seek an existence in the most appalling living and working conditions, to rise above this deprivation and squalor, to shape and make a better life for the whole of the working class.

The changes they brought about were lasting and eminently effective. One such person was Frederick Rogers, a bookbinder, who proves the point.

It is unknown whether Rogers had any formal education and he himself does not mention this in his autobiography entitled 'Labour, Life and Literature'. He does, however, tell us that he started work at the age of ten as an errand boy to an ironmonger. The hours were from eight to eight, Monday to Friday and eight a.m. to ten p.m. on a Saturday for a princely wage of two shillings a week.

From there he became a sandwich boy, which meant that he paraded the City of London with a billboard front and back announcing to all and sundry the virtues of a fire-proof safe. The immediate benefit was two hours less a day (which gave him reading time), and a 50 per cent increase in wages. In this way he got to know the City and its environs well.

In 1860, at the age of 14, he got a job with Rock Brothers and Payne, a City stationers, at 4s. 6d. a week. His job consisted mainly of warehousing, which meant carrying heavy bundles of paper from the ground floor, up narrow staircases, to the floors above, and on returning, bringing the finished work down.

In his own words he said, 'No work could be worse for a growing lad'.

Although the work was heavy and the hours long, the job had two distinct advantages. On the one hand it introduced Rogers to the industry in which he was to progress to become a vellum bookbinder, and on the other hand, it allowed him to utilise his lunch break and visit the numerous churches within the City and listen to the various preachers interpreting religion with the current political, economic and social problems.

Frederick Rogers.

Consequently, Rogers was to develop his own debating skills and knowledge. One must also add that it fed an increasing certainty to the making of a man with a great sense of political and social awareness.

Rogers, who had worked diligently as a warehouseman, then became apprenticed to a vellum bookbinder. This led him into the Vellum Bookbinders Trade Society (1806), in which he was to play an important and historical role. His love of reading and seeking of knowledge were eventually to make him a most respected and acknowledged literary figure in the trade union field of the day.

His crusades throughout the 80s were for the advancement of the pay and conditions of bookbinders and the elimination of the sweat-shops, together with universal education for the working class. As well as being an accomplished speaker, Rogers was increasingly becoming a proliferate pamphleteer.

1891 saw the bookbinders on strike in an attempt to achieve the eight hour day. It was during this strike that he wrote the following appeal:

> 'In order to put some of their unemployed comrades in work, it is a new departure and in making it the binders have shown that labour is influenced by higher ethical principles than capital, that it is along these lines of labour movements that the moral evolution of the race will proceed.
>
> 'Vellum binders everywhere, help us fight for a man's claim to live a man's life, for leisure in which to think of other things than bread alone, for a chance to help our fellows into work, for time to realise that we are not mere beasts of burden, doomed to work forever from morning till night to make other men rich, but human beings with immortal souls who are claiming the right to live a human life. We are for principle, not pocket money.' 19. 12. 1891.

In March, after 20 weeks on strike the binders were forced to return to work without achieving their objective. Worse, however, was that the funds of the union were so depleted that if another member had died and the death benefit been paid, the union would have been insolvent.

It was in that year, 1892, that Rogers was elected President of the Vellum Bookbinders, a position in which he was to have a marked impact.

His first task was to break the monopoly of the two firms who did Her Majesty's Stationery Office work. By writing letters to newspapers and getting questions asked in Parliament, on the evidence that Rogers had gathered, the Government of the day were put on the defensive. He then led delegations to the Home Secretary and in this way gave good effect to the Fair Wages Resolution that was to be a great ally of all trade unions for the next 90 years.

Following this, in 1893, Rogers was proud to say that, 'Probably the Bookbinders was the only union with no unemployed members'.

It was also in 1892 that Rogers attended his first TUC, which was held in Glasgow, and again, quoting his own words:

> 'I saw in a flash that it was going to be a training ground for the Labour politicians and that it might become a larger and more enlightened ground than that which had trained Liberalism and developed the democratic idea generally.
>
> 'My week in Glasgow stirred new ideas in my mind, it was a week of vision as well as practical work.'

On his return Rogers was to write:

> 'I was there on the eve of great constitutional changes in the life of Congress, and this I did not know. My trade had not been represented at Congresses for many years, I had everything to learn. The old trade unions and the new were in sharp conflict. Labour movements have often had larger outlooks than seats.
>
> 'The Parliament of Labour, like the Parliament at Westminster, discussed questions of the day with as much acumen and as much fairness of judgement as in the House of Commons. Why should they not be? The Trade Unionist, like the co-operator, is getting educated in the duties of citizenship through the organisation to which he belongs. Under all the talk there was seen to be an earnest,

honest purpose, that of helping Labour to get its fair share of the fruits of its work. Regarded as a phase in the development of the Democratic idea the Congress was in every way hopeful and encouraging. It was dominated by a high ideal of justice.'

This was 'meat and drink' to Rogers. His distrust of the middle class was intense, he believed that only the working class could alone resolve their own destiny. It was thus that he wrote to Lansbury:

'A Labour Party in the House of Commons strong enough to compel the respect of either Party (Tory and Liberal), and strong enough to hold the balance of power would put an end to the power of landowners and capitalists. If only the working class will strive for this, better times will be had for them and theirs.'

In 1893 Rogers attended the first annual meeting of the Independent Labour Party, which was held in Bradford. Rogers disliked it because of the large middle class element in it, but saw it had possibilities.

In February 1900, he attended the inaugural conference of the Labour Representation Committee on behalf of the Vellum Binders. There were 22 candidates for the seven trade unionists to sit on the executive, Rogers polled seventh place and was, therefore, elected. At the first meeting he was voted into the chair and thereby Frederick Rogers earned the distinction of being the first chairman of the Labour Party.

In 1902/3 Rogers was Party Treasurer and in 1903 he wrote: 'Liberalism is nothing but a string of negatives, a universal "don't".'

It was because of this conviction that Rogers worked hard to prevent infiltration into the new party by middle class careerists.

It was, however, the fight for old age pensions that earned Rogers his greatest distinction. The campaign had been in existence some 20 years when in 1899 he was appointed the committee's secretary. It was called the National Committee of Organised Labour, and his term of office was to last 10 years.

He was, according to contemporaries, indefatigable in his efforts to secure state pensions. He travelled the length and breadth of the British Isles, holding forth at speaking engagements to all who cared to listen. He wrote 15 pamphlets and two had a publication of half a million copies each.

Ten years, however, is a long time and with all his other public work Rogers wrote to Ramsay MacDonald:

'My work has carried me all over the country, and pretty well worn me out, indeed I am so sick of the strain and the unreality of the "atmosphere" of every kind of public work that but for the fact that I really do want some results to come from my agitation on behalf of old age pensions it would take me no time to chuck over everything and go back to the bench again. If the workman only knew it, his position is very much more honourable than that of the public agitator. But I have no record of failure to write after my public agitation, in fact, it has been a tremendous success.' 18.11.1902.

It was with the backcloth of the Poor Law and the knowledge of the 'workhouse' (into which the destitute were put, where husband was separated from wife, wife from children, and the place made inhospitable to discourage 'layabouts') that fired Rogers' conscience and sustained him. From his own experience he knew that when age and infirmity had taken its toll, for a worker who could no longer be 'gainfully'

JOHN BULL'S CREDITORS.

WORKMAN. "How about my Dwelling's Bill?
SCHOOL-BOARD SCHOLAR. "I want my breakfast."
OLD WORKMAN. "Where's that old Age Pension?"
STARVING INDIAN. "What Mister Bull goin' to do for me?"

JOSEPH C. "Mr Bull can't attend to any of you now. He's absent on pressing business in South Africa."

SOCIALISM. "Well friends, you might as well ask for the whole loaf as for half. My little account covers all of yours & more, & it must be settled. In the mean time let us keep LABOUR DAY.

Political cartoon W. Crane.

employed, after a life-time of labour, much of it sweated, destitution and degradation were life's reward.

In 1908, Frederick Rogers' tireless work bore fruit. The then Liberal Government placed old age pensions on the statute book at five shillings a week.

It is remarkable that Rogers suffered ill health throughout his life yet worked so diligently on various different matters simultaneously.

An insight can be gained by the following account. A Dr John Watkins lived at 2 Falcon Square in the City of London (probably near Farringdon Street) and the good and kindly doctor had a great reputation for healing 'diseases of the bone'. He was also a philanthropist, treating the poor free of charge during certain hours of the day.

He was 78 years of age when Rogers first went to the surgery, and the doctor informed Rogers that he had never seen a case of spinal disease quite like it before, and he did not know that he could do much for him. If, however, he persevered and came frequently, the doctor would do his best. Thus, at the age of 20, Rogers found hope for his crippling disease and regularly walked the three miles to be at the doctor's at 5 a.m. in the morning, and from there to be at his bench at 7.30.

Four years of treatment were to restore him to lead an active life, although he was never completely cured and suffered his disability with continuing pain throughout his life. During this period, the doctor-patient relationship grew into a personal friendly climate in which Watkins, with his interests in science and religion, was to open a whole new world, strange and curious, in which Rogers could only listen open-mouthed.

Watkins loaned Rogers books as well as having long discussions with him, which Rogers found immensely valuable. Later on, when the old doctor grew feeble, and had failing eyesight, Rogers called on him and read him religious tracts and matters on science.

Robert Banner.

Keir Hardie's election agent

Robert Banner was born in 1855 in the City of Edinburgh. He joined the Edinburgh Branch of the Bookbinders' and Machine Rulers' Consolidated Union (1872) in 1877, and served within the branch and represented the Bookbinders on the Edinburgh Trades Council.

Quite early in his career he became a convinced socialist. In 1881 he was present at a conference held in Hamilton for the purpose of drawing up a definite socialist programme. Some claim that to this conference the present socialist movement in Great Britain owes its origin.

Leaving Edinburgh with the expressed intention of emigrating to America, Banner made his way to London. Here he was persuaded by his friend, Andreas Scheu, to remain and make London his home.

In London Banner soon found many congenial spirits. Among his intimate friends he counted William Morris, H. M. Hyndman, E. Belfort Bax, G. B. Shaw, Annie Besant, Eleanor Marx Aveling and many other leading socialists and reformers.

He became a prominent member of the SDF, was on the executive of the Fabian Society, and also on the executive of the Legal Eight Hours Committee.

Keir Hardie, the first Labour MP.

His activities were ceaseless. In 1892, when Keir Hardie was first returned to Parliament for South-West Ham, Robert Banner was his election agent, and to the strenuous exertions of the latter the success was largely due.

In 1895 Banner was elected a member of the Woolwich Board of Health, the governing body of the Woolwich Polytechnic, as a representative of the Technical Education Board of the LCC and he achieved the distinction of being elected a member of the Woolwich Borough Council. He contested the most reactionary ward in the borough, and was returned at the top of the poll.

From August, 1902, Robert Banner represented the London Branch at the General Council meeting and was a member of the London Branch Committee.

THE
LABOURER'S SONG

'Tis true our home's a cottage home,
Of wealth we cannot boast;
We cannot speak of house and land,
Of titled rank; the most
That we can claim is honest worth,
Combined with noble thought;
Yet these are things wealth seldom owns,
And titles never bought.

And yet, methinks, we still may hope,
In this fair world of ours,
With manly toil and frugal care,
To cull its sweetest flowers;
We'll hear the lark at early morn,
Kind thoughts shall cheer the day;
At night, the voice of other times,
Shall chase all gloom away.

And, though our home's a cottage home,
Whatever may befall,
We'll seek to scatter light and thought,
To illume that path of all –
Of all who struggle for the true,
Who battle with the wrong,
They shall bring truth uppermost –
The false was never strong.

Manchester   *Joseph Hutton*
26th March, 1863

9

The Printers' Labourers' Strike 1889

Brother, exert thy noblest powers,
Time will not be always ours,
Then let us labour while we may
And give to life a brighter day.

THIS chapter concerns the early beginnings of NATSOPA – now part of SOGAT '82 – and the struggle to form the early Society. It was a period of the successful fight of the gas workers for an 8-hour day, the Great Dock Strike, and the celebrated and bitter struggle of the match girls in the East End of London.

NATSOPA was first known as the Printers' Labourers' Union and this chapter indicates the injustices suffered by the unorganised workers outside the craft areas which brought forth the 'new unionism'.

NATSOPA was born in 1889, the year which will forever be memorable in the history of the trade union movement as the date of the great Dock Strike in London.

It was a time of ferment. The clash between the 'old unionism' and the 'new unionism' was at its height. The socialist crusaders – Hyndman, Morris, Bax and Quelch – had after eight years' propaganda begun to make some impression on the trade union movement.

The Fabians had just issued their famous 'Essays', and, in the North, Keir Hardie had stood as Independent Labour candidate for Mid-Lanark in the by-election of 1888. The trade depression of previous years had given way to rising prosperity and the time was ripe for a widespread forward movement.

Just when the dockers were on the verge of victory, and inspired no doubt by their gallant stand for justice, a number of printers' labourers employed by the firm of Spottiswoode and Company asked for an increase in wages. What those wages were is set out in the manifesto issued a few weeks later.

'Our present wages' it declares, 'vary from 12s. to 14s. per week, and many among us have wives and families to sustain. We work on an average 54 hrs. a week and 75 hrs. to earn £1.'

The conditions in which printers' labourers worked were wretched in the extreme. The manifesto asserts that their employers 'would not put their pet cats and dogs in the styes where they condemn us to pass our best working years . . . in heated cellars where gaslight replaces daylight, midst perpetual din, breathing a stifling, filthy atmosphere . . . We have to keep hand and eye ever on the alert to keep stroke with the machines we tend.'

In order to earn this meagre reward of £1 in 75 hours a man had to put in a stretch of 36 hours continuous labour, and the effect on health and stamina may be imagined. The overtime rates varied from 3d. to 5d. per hour, while casual labour was paid at the rate of 2s. 6d. to 3s. per day.

The immediate result of the workers' demand was that Messrs. Spottiswoode flatly refused to grant any concession. The spark kindled by Messrs. Mike Vaughan, Tom Mansfield, Fred Quinn and 'Happy' Heighington, had, however, spread to other firms in the City.

Trade being brisk, several of these agreed to an advance of 5s. per week. The malcontents at Spottiswoode's thereupon determined to leave work. A council of war was held on a piece of waste ground adjoining Old Farringdon Market, opposite the firm's works, a strike committee was formed, and it was decided to carry on an agitation throughout the trade.

It was under these circumstances that the first banner of the incipient union came into existence. It was constructed of two broom handles, with a 'stroker' hanging at each end as ornaments, and between them a couple of yards of white calico bearing the inscription, 'We Demand One Pound Per Week, and Sixpence Per Hour Overtime.'

Headed by this banner, and occasionally by a band consisting of one tin whistle, the strikers visited various works, and in several instances succeeded either in inducing the employers to grant the increase demanded or in withdrawing the labourers.

Messrs. Spottiswoode were, however, still obdurate, and other firms were soon engaging hands at the old rates. Known agitators were put on the 'black list', and it was felt that the campaign must become more aggressive if eventual security of conditions was to be attained.

Accordingly, a meeting was called to consider the position. Amongst the score or so present were Messrs. J. Keep, T. Bastow, and 'Curly' King. Everyone agreed that the thing to do was to organise but who was to do the organising was not so clear – until a stranger to most of those present rose to speak.

Introduced by the chairman as a member of the London Society of Compositors and an active propagandist in the socialist movement, Mr George Evans so impressed the gathering with his qualifications that he was at once appointed secretary of a campaign committee. The first work of this committee was to draft and issue the manifesto referred to above, which called upon the printers' labourers to 'Strike . . . Strike all together . . . Stand together and win.'

The manifesto was issued in August, 1889, from the Red Star Coffee House, Clerkenwell Green. It was signed on behalf of the Printers' Strike Committee by George Evans and G. Walden.

On the third Monday in August this appeal brought out a large number of men, and by evening several firms had capitulated, but victory was still not in sight. The guerrilla warfare therefore went on. Propaganda of various kinds continued and funds subscribed by the more fortunate were distributed amongst the unemployed and the victimised.

A room was rented at 4 Wine Office Court, Fleet Street, and from this address Mr George Evans, the first secretary, announced that on Saturday, September 16th, the office would be open for the enrolment of members at an entrance fee of 1s. So far, free cards had been issued broadcast, and about 2,000 were in circulation. Now came the acid test.

Alas, the expected crowd of applicants did not materialise. Between 9.30 a.m. and 3 p.m. not more than 40 cards were issued, and news was received that secret agents of the employers had been at work among the men, inducing them to return to work at 18s. per week, and no guarantee as to the rate for overtime.

Nothing daunted by this set-back, Mr George Evans and a few stalwarts undertook a house-to-house canvass and roped 200 converts into the fold. By the end of October the membership had increased to 500, and, where solidarity existed, no man without the union card was allowed to work. Nevertheless, quite 50 per cent of the firms were paying wages below the minimum. There was still a long row to hoe.

The weekly subscription of 2d. per member was barely sufficient to meet general expenses, and even had the rules permitted, quite inadequate to provide dispute benefit. Consequently, the organisation had to depend on voluntary contributions, and though the stalwarts responded generously men in dispute frequently had to go home with much less than the old minimum.

TO PRINTERS' LABOURERS

AND OTHER WORKERS IN THE PRINTING TRADE

We, the Printers' Labourers, are on strike for a wage of **20s. per Week** and 6d. per hour overtime. We appeal to the Machine Minders and other workers to aid us in obtaining our just demands.

Our present wages vary from **12s. to 14s. per week,** and many among us have wives and families to sustain. We work on an average fifty-four hours a week, and

SEVENTY-FIVE HOURS TO EARN £1.

How, and under what conditions do we work? In heated cellars where gaslight replaces daylight; amidst perpetual din; breathing a stifling, filthy atmosphere. We have to keep eye and hand ever on the alert to **KEEP STROKE** with the machines we tend.

Our kind, respectable Christian employers would not put their pet cats and dogs in the styes where they condemn us to pass our best working years. Above are the demands for the toil which destroys our health

We appeal to all fellow labourers to join us. Do not listen to the specious talk of interested foremen and employers who **"promise to favourably consider your demands."** They want time to work off urgent orders. If you on strike are selfish enough to go in because a few employers grant concessions, you help to ruin the cause. Will you purchase your gain at the expense of our defeat? Show the same spirit as our comrades in other industries are displaying.

STRIKE !!

STRIKE ALL TOGETHER !!

Stand Together and Win

Printers' Strike Committee,

RED STAR COFFEE HOUSE, CLERKENWELL GREEN.

GEORGE EVANS, *Sec.*
GEORGE WALDEN, *Treas.*

It was therefore determined to issue an appeal for financial assistance, but this itself was an anxious problem. To print it would cost money. Would it pay?

Bright brains soon found a solution. Residing with Mr. Martin Hanness, one of the old brigade, was a printers' labourer, Mr Tom Clerihew, a middle-aged man with a turn for engineering. In his spare time he made a small printing press, and had collected a complete case of type.

The plant was taken to Wine Office Court. Mr George Evans set up the type, whilst Messrs J. Keep and C. Crawley took charge of the press. Printing ink and roller were found to be lacking, but enterprising scouts soon discovered sources of supply, and the job was run off, although no machine minder was present to make ready.

The result of this appeal was most encouraging, particularly in the case of London Compositors, who established weekly collections in their chapels, and recommended the appeal to their Council, which responded handsomely with a donation of £21. The union put new vigour into the campaign against the employers, and the membership increased to such an extent that expenses were more than covered.

Spottiswoode and Company were, however, still recalcitrant, but it was decided to postpone further action in their case until a really favourable opportunity should occur.

Early in February, 1890, the first official general meeting of the Printers' Labourers' Union was held at the Hop Exchange School of Arms, SE. At this meeting were present a group of malcontents who had a few months earlier raided the office and threatened violence if they were not allowed to inspect the books.

Again they voiced their complaints, but the officers who had been acting provisionally thoroughly vindicated their conduct of affairs, and were elected with acclamation. The first financial statement showed a balance in hand of £36.

Following this gathering a series of Sunday evening concerts and socials was organised, and a banner fund was opened, which brought in £17. The ceremony of unfurling the banner took place at the Victoria Hall, SE, where a first-class variety entertainment was arranged. The banner was unfurled by Messrs W. M. Thompson and W. Steadman, and the function was a great success, the funds benefiting to the amount of £150.

The financial position being so healthy the officials decided to proceed with the movement against Spottiswoode and Company. At first conciliatory methods were adopted. Mr George Evans wrote pointing out that most firms were paying the 20s. minimum and 6d. per hour overtime, and requesting Spottiswoode's to come into line.

1889 surviving members reunion meeting 1929.

To everyone's surprise, the firm at once agreed to comply, and the following Friday the increase was granted. At the same time, six of the most prominent men in the chapel received notices to leave.

This extraordinary action resulted in the withdrawal of the whole of the members, the firm refusing either explanation or satisfaction. The dispute was fought with vigour by both sides, and many exciting incidents occurred between the union's pickets and the blackleg labour imported by the firm, some of which ended in the police court.

At the end of three months, however, the union was compelled to strike its flag, but the struggle was not all loss, the event being followed by an influx of members and an improvement in the finances. Some of the men who took part in this dispute obtained situations elsewhere.

BRITANNIA'S BEST DEFENCE
AGAINST HER WORST ENEMY.
DEDICATED TO ALL TRUE LOVERS OF THEIR COUNTRY
BY WALTER CRANE.

Political Poster W. Crane.

90

10

The Women of the Salle – Annie Bridge & Miss Smith

'The splendours of the firmament of time
May be eclipsed, but are extinguished not;
Like stars to their appointed height they climb.
And death is a low mist, which cannot blot
The brightness it may veil.'

ANNIE Bridges was born in Radcliffe, Lancashire on 29th June, 1883. By her thirteenth year she was working at the East Lancashire Paper Mill, Radcliffe, where she worked in the 'Salle' for the next 17 years. Within the records of this company appears a reference to a No. 255 A. Parkes (Maiden Name) on 11th March, 1897 giving her gross wage as 8 shillings and 1 penny for a week of 60 hours worked. When asked many years later what started her involvement with the Union she stated 'I revolted against women being obligated to work for 60 hours a week from 6.00 a.m. till 6.00 p.m. with one hour break within the day for breakfast and dinner and half an hour on Saturdays'. When in 1908 the Bury Branch Secretary of the old National Union of Printing, Bookbinding, Machine Ruling and Paper Workers visited the East Lancs. Paper Mill asking the women to attend a meeting all promised, but, because of fear, only three attended and of that number one joined – Mrs Bridge. Thus started not only a long and distinguished career, but she had become by 1914 the first woman organiser out of many that followed her within the National Union.

Annie married George Ralph Bridge on 7th November, 1908. He was by all accounts a kindly and the gentlest of men, though also having quite a reputation as an amateur boxer, working as a 'Beetler' in a dye works for £1.75 a week until the outbreak of the first World War when he joined the East Lancashire Regiment. As a sergeant of this regiment he was killed in action in the Battle of the Somme on 5th November, 1916, leaving Annie Bridge a widow with a young son Norman.

Annie, following the death of her husband, intensified her work as an official of the Union. Her early radicalism inherited from the early gatherings at her parents' home which were a mixture of musical entertainment (piano, violin and wind instruments, with much singing) and political argument assisted her then and for the next 29 years as an official of the Union.

It was said that she knew every papermill in the country, as well as most printing houses, from Kent to the North East and from South Wales and the South West to the North West. She used to stand outside mill gates (with her young son) in all weathers trying to organise, especially her first love 'The Women of the Salle'.

One story against the men she met which was often quoted – in one five-week spell in South Wales she lodged with a papermaker's family; it was a tiny house without much privacy and she noticed that the husband used to don a clean shirt each weekend 'but always on top of the old one'.

Many people in the Labour Movement of those early days also tried very hard on many occasions to get Annie to stand for Parliament, but her answer was always the same – that she had worked in a paper mill for 17 years and felt that her prime role in life was to keep trying to better the pay and conditions of those whose work she knew so well, as well as of the print workers who had come increasingly under her care. 'I know I can do this' she would say 'but in the wider field of parliamentary representation I might not feel so certain'.

Annie Bridge from Rabotshayn Gazette, USSR.

One of the greatest highlights of her life was as a representative of the TUC of an investigation by British Women Trade Unionists on Soviet Russia which took place, travelling over land between April and July 1925, the investigating team being the first British women Trades Unionists to visit Russia following the Revolution. On the return of a male Trade Union Delegation from Russia in 1924 it was generally felt that interesting as was their report, nevertheless the general impression of Russia at that time was incomplete in that the delegation had not included women, who it might be urged would be quick to appreciate conditions affecting the work, health and general conditions of women and children in Russia. Hence arose the idea of a

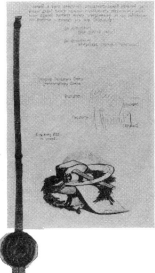

Translation of Address to the Delegates.　　　　　　　　　　　　　*Reproduced above.*

All-Russian Council of Trade Unions
GROZNY DISTRICT TRADE UNION COUNCIL

Workers of the World, Unite!

Long Live the Unity of the Trade Union Movement of the World!

Long Live the International Unity of the Working Class!

THE workers of Grozny extend a hearty comradely welcome to the British working women's delegation and are sincerely glad that their British comrades will see, once again, through the eyes of this delegation, all that we have done, are doing, and all that still remains to be done, to reorganise the country on a Socialist basis.

The Soviet workers in general, and the Grozny workers in particular, are delighted with the visit of our dear guests – the British working women delegation – because it will give the latter an opportunity to see for themselves, and once again to tell the exact truth about us, to our British working class comrades. They will relate all that they see of which they approve as well as all that they may not approve. The Soviet workers desire, above all, that their foreign comrades should know the real truth of all their achievements and of all the difficulties under which they labour in the building up of their Workers' and Peasants' State. They are constructing this State without the landowners and bourgeoisie, using only their own horny hands of toil. In this work, the Soviet workers are buoyed up by the faith that sooner or later the workers will be victorious the whole world over.

The best hope of the inevitable triumph of the workers of the world over capitalism, is the close relations established between the British and Soviet workers. For this will form a firm basis for the united front of the workers of the world against the capitalists. It will be by the united front, which will undoubtedly be established sooner or later, that the workers of the world will eventually overthrow capitalism in spite of the reign of terror whereby the latter hopes to cow and defeat the workers.

Inspire with the belief in the imminent triumph of world labour over world capitalism, the Grozny workers say to their dear visitors: "We are delighted to welcome you here. We have no doubt, that after investigating life in the first Soviet Socialist country of the world, you will do everything possible on your return home to further the extension and consolidation of the United Front of the Trade Union Movement, thus bringing nearer the real fraternity and liberation of the workers of the world."

Long Live our Guests!

Long Live the British Men and Women Workers!

Presidium of the Grozny Trade Union Council

Chairman:
A. NASLEDOV.

Secretary:
I. AKSELBANT.

Grozny, June 11, 1925.

women's delegation. This delegation consisted of four delegates representing the printing, garment workers, textile trades and a representative of the transport and general workers. It was accompanied by an advisory delegate and clerical secretary, both women.

The delegation left England on 23rd April, arriving in Moscow on the morning of 27th April. On 30th April, two of the delegates went to Leningrad to witness the May Day celebrations in that town. On 3rd May, the rest of the delegation left Moscow for Leningrad, stopping there until 8th May, after which the whole delegation returned to Moscow, stopping at Tver for one day. After spending a few more days in Moscow, the whole delegation left for Kharkov, visiting subsequently the Crimea, Balaclava, Sebastopol, Rostov-on-Don, Kislovodsk, Grozny, Baku, Tiflis, Borzhom, Abas-Tuman, and by way of the Georgian Military Road, to Vladikavkaz, whence it went back direct to Moscow, and after spending a few more days there, left for England, arriving in London on 4th July.

From the moment when the delegation arrived in Riga and was met by the Soviet Ambassador and women representatives of the All-Russian Council of Trade Unions, it received every facility and assistance for carrying out its work of investigation. On arrival in Moscow the delegation intimated the exact purpose of its visit to the USSR and the main institutions and industries as well as the parts of the country it desired to visit, an approximate programme was then drawn up by the representatives of the All-Russian Council of Trade Unions which the delegation freely discussed and altered to suit its requirements. A similar procedure was followed in every town visited by the delegation. Whilst the local trade union and Soviet Authorities made suggestions, it was the delegation itself who decided where they should go, and what they should see, the authorities always providing all the necessary facilities.

Beginning with the Sebezh frontier, the delegation was met everywhere with the greatest enthusiasm and friendliness by the workers. In every town they visited, the

May Day Parade, Leningrad, 1925. 600,000 workers marched past.

delegation was overwhelmed by invitations from workers to visit their factories and their clubs. Red Army soldiers, officers and sailors, requested visits to their headquarters, clubs and exercise grounds. Teachers wished them to visit their schools; nurses and doctors put in claims for health institutions, such as sanatoria, rest homes, and hospitals. The children, particularly the Young Pioneers, were to the fore in every demonstration with their bands and their revolutionary songs, which either called to battle or were reminiscent of the bad old days, and asked them to visit their own special functions. Children from the Children's Homes came and begged a visit to their particular home, and were evidently keenly disappointed when the delegation was, as often happened, compelled to refuse, owing to lack of time.

There exist today many photographs and Annie's day by day notes and observations of this visit.

An example of notes written by Annie Bridge during her visit

26th April, 1925

At Riga we were met by the Russian Ambassador and put into a state coach fitted with a saloon and every convenience, better sleeping accommodation and more space.

28th April, 1925

Visited textile factory where in 1905 workers were marched outside, placed against the wall and shot for asking for better conditions, 7,500 workers employed.

1st May, 1925 (11.00 a.m.)
Arrived Leningrad

Drive to Grandstand in front of Winter Palace, 600,000 workers march past, with tableaux, bands and effigies representing the various trades and former conditions compared with present developments in industries, prisons, priests, bishops, 1,000 girls and youths showing physical culture, kiddies homes. Demonstration lasted until 5.30 p.m. Evening, Opera House Show, Red Petrograd, staging the story of the revolution, showing how the present Red Army was first formed by the workers from the workshops, play supervised by workers who had taken part in the revolution – most realistic.

8th May, 1925

On the 8th we visited the Czars Village now called the Children's Village as during the revolution, kiddies were congregated there for safety. There were rooms of amber, Wedgewood Marble, pink and white and green, mosaic pictures, silk damask walls, silver baths, Japanese room, inlaid pearl furniture, blue and purple marble columns.

13th May, 1925

On the 13th instant we attended the opening of the 3rd Congress of the USSR

5 Commisariats
- Finance
- Railways
- Postal & Telegraph
- Commerce & Industry
- Foreign Affairs

Visitors from Turkistan request to be allowed to join the Soviets, also Turcomain, Taschish, Kuban and Don Cossacks, formerly National Republics.

14th May, 1925

We paid a visit to the Kremlin which we found very interesting but not furnished in so grand a way as the Czars village palace, we found huge crystal vases, marble tables, natural wood floors, white marble walls, Japanese porcelain.

22nd May, 1925

Leaving Kharkov we then went to Artermosk or Bakmut in the Donetz Basin. We were taken to see a salt mine. In the district were 300,000 workers, 130,000 miners, 40,000 metal, 15,000 chemical 115,000 bld., food and general. 92% of these were organised, the rest being peasants from the villages. Down the salt mine we found columns of salt 102 ft. thick left in order to prevent sinking. Here we were presented with a paper weight and blotter made of salt. The roads were terribly bad through the rain and we had a very unusual experience.

It was not just a fraternal journey, for her notes indicate not hundreds of people turned out to meet them, but thousands, which she remembered until the end of her days. Her report ends with the following observations:

> In giving our report of what we saw and learned during our visit to Soviet Russia, we are not at all concerned with the question as to the righteousness of the Bolsheviks, or as to their methods of establishing the soviet system. In investigating conditions in a foreign country we have to take institutions as we find them, and only two things concern us: firstly, is that system accepted by the majority of the people who live under it? secondly, does it on the whole work out for the benefit of the toiling masses of the country? We say quite frankly that we are definitely and all the time on the side of our own class, the exploited working class (including working peasants and both brain and hand workers).

Annie worked more and more in the North East as the Union grew during the 1930's and 1940's and retired during the second World War in 1943. She lived in retirement in the Lake District until she died at the age of 87 years in 1970, still remembered by many and never to be forgotten.

Saved from a life of sin

In the year 1909 three years after her appointment as Female Section Organiser, Miss Smith the first recorded Woman Organiser gave an interview in the March edition of 'The Printers Assistant'. This journal was the official organ of The Society of Printers and Assistants later known as NATSOPA, now amalgamated into SOGAT '82. The context of this interview was as follows:

The choice fell upon Miss Smith, who took up the duties of her office some three years ago, and a better selection could not have been made.

She came to the service of the society with practical knowledge of the trade, having been employed by three London firms in various capacities; and with experience of organising work, having done good service in connection with the organisation of the women and girls employed in the baking industry of Paris.

It was no mere apprentice, therefore, that was called to do the organising of the female workers in the interests of the society and of industrial unity, but a woman of experience.

She knows the needs of the worker, for she has felt them; and there is no one who more fully appreciates the necessity of union if the conditions of the worker, male and female, are to be made better.

To anyone visiting Miss Smith in her little sanctum at Caxton House as I was privileged to do the other day the first impression conveyed is that one is in the presence of an earnest woman, who seeks the good of her fellow women, and who knows no other way to secure it than by unity.

Womanlike, Miss Smith has a weakness for tea, which she makes excellently well, and over our cups we discussed the question of female organisation generally, but in relation to the NSOPA in particular.

'How does the work affect you, Miss Smith?'

'I find it hard, and almost unending, for an Organiser has generally to act by day and think by night. It is this latter that wears one. You can never forget your work, and every faculty of body and mind is constantly in exercise. To be tactful here, forbearing there, and more forceful somewhere else; to see where you may have been in error to-day, and try to remedy it to-morrow; to be misunderstood by some, misrepresented by others, and to be met by disappointments and disillusionments at every turn – these are the experiences of an Organiser, and yet the life has its compensations, and one has always the satisfaction of knowing that one is working for good.'

'You began your work for the NSOPA at Tonbridge, I think?'

'I have been the instrument of rescuing from a vicious life, 175 of those girls'
Miss Smith, first woman organiser.

'I did, and there, as everywhere else, I have found the women and girls ready to be organised. I mean they were conscious of the disadvantages and injustice under which they live, and yet reluctant to take the decisive step. One deterrent, no doubt, is the claim that joining a society would make on the miserable wages they receive.

'Some of them do not earn – I mean receive – more than 3s. to 5s. per week, and a payment of even 3d. out of that constitutes a tax; another deterrent is the fear of the 'boss' or overseer, which is continually before their eyes. They are afraid that association with a society such as ours would mean an immediate strike on their part, or a lock-out on the part of the employers if the association were known, and either would mean disaster to them.'

'And how do you meet their objections?'

'Well, I try to get them to understand that they are indispensable to the masters, who are not philanthropists when work and wages are in question. They are cheaper than men, but there is no reason even at present why they should be so much cheaper. It may be that we cannot get the wages brought up to the level of the male rate, but we can raise the present level and that will be a step toward the higher wage.

Destitute women – H. J. Pugh.

'I urge this on the ground that the effort should be made in justice to themselves and in justice to the male workers, who suffer on account of the underpaid females. But all this can only be brought by combination. The salvation of the workers lies in that way.'

'And the employers, how do you find them in your dealings with them?'

'I have almost invariably found them courteous to me personally. It is with the foremen and overseers I have had most trouble. But all through I have found that if there is one thing the employers are opposed to more than another it is the union of the women workers. They will make any promise to prevent combination, and any to get those out of it who are already in.

'It is a rather delicate subject to broach, but may I ask you, Miss Smith, whether you have formed any opinion of the morality of the girls whose interests you look after? I ask this because the Rev. Mr Campbell, of the City Temple, has said and maintains, that in another industry, the low wages paid to the girls force them –'.

'I know what you mean, and have read what Mr Campbell has said. Of the industry to which he refers I cannot speak, but of the industry with which I am connected I can, and if Mr Campbell's knowledge is equal to my own experience, I can endorse every word of his. Good heavens! How can it be otherwise? Pay a girl from 3s. to 5s. a week – a single girl – how can she live on it? It is not a subject upon which I care to enlarge.

"All I need say is that while I have not found many cases of open prostitution, I have found too many cases in which the insufficient wage paid by the employer have led to a course of life equally bad. In passing from this subject may I just say that I have never lost sight of this side of the industrial question, and it has been my supreme pleasure to have been, in ways I need not say, the instrument of rescuing from a vicious life 175 of those girls.'

'You have been very good to me, Miss Smith. Will you just tell me before I go, whether you are satisfied with your work of three years?'

'If you mean with the results, judged by the roll of membership, no. If you mean by the efforts I have made, the conscientious work I have put in, yes. Perhaps another will reap where I have sown, but I have sown what I believe to be good seed. In my dealings with the female workers I have never allowed myself to think that I am merely operating upon materials out of which Trade Unionists may be made.

'The making of unionists is no doubt my business, but that can best be done by making friends of the women and girls, and I am glad to say that I can look upon my members as my personal friends. I try to cultivate this personal friendship, and my life has known few higher gratifications than have come into it from the sympathetic bond which unites many of my members to me. To many of them life has been hard, and to some of them a true human sympathetic touch has rarely come.

'I have tried to give that touch of sympathy where it was needed, and to be a guide and adviser to them, as woman can be to woman, and I like to think that a tie stronger than that of Trade Unionism binds us together, and the relationship makes better women and better workers, as well as better Trade Unionists of us.'

The position of Organiser of the Women's Section was introduced in 1906 and Miss Smith was appointed to this position. She had been doing the work for several months before that.

She started in Tonbridge and organised a section there. In the next few months she visited up to ten other provincial centres and a branch was formed in each centre. She then organised females in several London firms and in 1907 had her most successful year, but this was marred by her own breakdown through overwork. Six new branches were opened.

In 1909 the post of Female Organiser was abolished and Mr J. Norey was chosen as Organiser. Miss Smith was the sister of Edwin Smith, General Secretary of the National Society of Printers and Assistants 1899–1909.

THE COLD HAS PASSED AWAY

Cold winter, with its chilly winds
Has left us for awhile,
And spring-time, with its newborn flowers,
Makes hills and valleys smile;
And many a home is cheerful now,
And many a heart is gay,
For spring has brought us sunny warmth-
'The cold has passed away.'

Once more the lark's sweet song is heard,
Once more the fields are green,
And all around where flow'rets bloom,
Bright joyous life is seen;
And with the earliest dawn of light,
Forgetful of decay,
The peasant sings his labour song-
'The cold has passed away.'

Bright summer-time will visit us,
And autumn with its store
Of fruit and grain will come again,
As welcome as of yore;
And workers in the world's broad field
Must remember still that they-
Who nobly win, can truly sing-
'The cold has passed away.'

Manchester   *Joseph Hutton*
26th April, 1862

11

Why we were celebrating on 28th June

With flow'ry June our festal day
Shall ever welcome prove,
Like summer's breath upon our hearts,
Our joyous feelings move.
Rejoice to-day, be blithe and gay,
And memory's pride renew.

ON Tuesday, 28th June, 1983, SOGAT '82 celebrated its 200th anniversary as a Trade Society. Many of our earlier forefathers were charged for various offences deemed by the state as treasonable acts under the Combination Laws, in force during the early days of our 'beginnings'.

Mr Henry Aston, of Nottingham
(60 Years' Member of the
B. & M.R.C.U.).

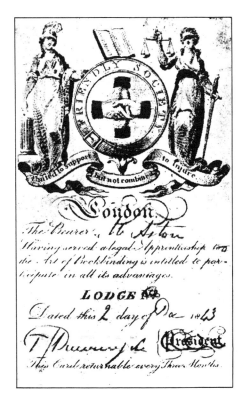

Note also the blindfold on the scales of justice.

June 28th was, for nearly a century, celebrated by the old Consolidated Union throughout the trade to commemorate the release of four of the 'Five Martyrs' – the bookbinder 'Men of the Combination' – from Newgate Gaol on the 28th June, 1788. They had served 14 months of a two-year sentence, one dying in prison of gaol fever. They were sentenced for striking against their masters and asking for an hour off the working day.

At a similar Anniversary Celebration 75 years later, held by the Nottingham, Derby and Leicester Branches who united together to celebrate the occasion, a long-serving member of the Nottingham Branch, a Mr Henry Aston, said: 'I am requested to say a few words explanatory of this Jubilee – to answer that question is to relate the following story.'

> It is related of Peter Cunningham (Nineteenth Century Naturalist) that when travelling the wilds of Australia he carried peach stones in his pocket and, when passing barren places, he flung them 'broadcast'. These same stones, alighting upon genial soil became, in the course of a few years, fine trees; and many travellers, wearied and parched, have refreshed themselves from the fruit of these trees, and testified to the usefulness of Cunningham's labours. Now, what he did in the natural world, our forefathers in our own trades did in the social world, they set the seed, and we reaped the fruit.

We today, in the twentieth century, by comparing our present position with that of our forefathers, and the Consolidated Union members of that 75th year of celebration, know that even in the present economic recession we are by comparison infinitely better off.

Indeed in a general description of all trades published in the eighteenth century it says: 'The working hours is from 6 o'clock in the morning till nine o'clock in the evening', an illustration of the daily working hours expected of many trades of the time. To ask for less, to strike for less, or to combine together to achieve less, were considered to be acts of treason against the state and the masters.

A POET'S WISH

> *I would not wish thee wealth, my friend,*
> *I would not wish thee fame,*
> *I'd wish thee something better far,*
> *Than an empty, sounding name; –*
> *A love for all that's truly good*
> *And worthy of esteem,*
> *A noble life, with thoughts as pure*
> *And sweet as an angel's dream.*

Manchester   *Joseph Hutton*
26th September, 1863.

The above poem was written, along with many others, by Joseph Hutton. In 1863 he was chairman of the old Consolidated Union of Bookbinders, and at a similar celebration that year was reported as saying:

> That nothing could give him greater pleasure than he felt on meeting a body of his fellow-workmen, meeting together as they were to commemorate such an important event in the Consolidated Union's Trade History.

Unfortunately, within three years of this statement he died at the early age of 44 years, the cause of which can only be put down to the untiring effort for the movement and the tragic circumstances which developed within his family.

The first photograph of a Bookbinders' Union delegate meeting – August 1864. Back row (l. to r.): J. Millar, J. Grant, H. McPhail, R. McCarthy, J. Mustart, W. Smith, J. Roy. Middle row: R. King, R. Brown, J. Rigby, H. Aston. Front row: C. Bacon, M. Oliver, W. Timbs, J. Hutton, G. Owen, C. S. J. Hewitt.

This can be illustrated by quoting his obituary within the Minutes of The Consolidated Union of June 1866:

OBITUARY

It is with deep regret we have to record the death of Mr Joseph Hutton, who departed this life on the first day of May, 1866, aged 44 years. In the loss of Mr Hutton the Union is deprived of one of its most sincere, hardworking, and useful members; one who was ever ready to devote his time and abilities, and make almost any sacrifice to gain an object or further the interest of his fellow-workmen. He will be remembered by most of our members as the chairman of the Central Committee, and afterwards their treasurer, in which capacities he was most assiduous in his attention to the duties of the offices he held, candid, honest, and straightforward in all his trans-actions, always anxious and persevering in anything he took in hand. Mr Hutton will also be remembered as the Manchester delegate and chairman at the late delegate meeting; indeed there has been no important question before the Union for the past few years in which he has not taken a lively interest, and in discussion, by his thorough good sense, sound judgment, and eloquence, has often brought a difficult subject to a peaceful and satisfactory conclusion.

The last great work of his life, in connection with the trade, was the assistance he rendered in the 'Short-Time Movement' in Manchester. It was mainly owing to the untiring exertions of Mr Hutton that the success of that movement was due. He attended the soiree held to celebrate the event, which was the last time he appeared among his fellow-tradesmen, being prostrated on a bed of sickness a few days afterwards; when after a long and protracted illness he died. The visitations which have, during a brief period, befallen Mr Hutton's family have been of the most heart-rending description: four of his fine healthy children having been, since November last, sacrificed to that dreadful scourge of the human race – scarlet fever. One after another were carried away to their grave; but his trials were borne with exemplary patience till his pet son, Edwin, fell a victim, when his cup of sorrow seemed full to the brim: he lost all fortitude and gradually sunk, leaving a wife and orphan son to mourn his loss.

June 1866

Joseph Hutton's endeavours outlined in the 'obituary' in the 'Short-Time Movement', along with many others, became a reality in January of 1866, when the Consolidated Union adopted and stated within its minutes, 'We are endeavouring to obtain an advance in wages; there is little fear but we will succeed in gaining it, now that trade is good; but in our opinion it would have been much better to have taken up the 'Short-Hour Movement', as by general reduction in the hours of work labour, it becomes more value'. The Hours Movement reaped its reward in the end.

THERE'S SOMETHING STILL WORTH LIVING FOR

by Joseph Hutton, bookbinder

There's something still worth living for
In this old world of ours,
Though soon its brightest lights depart
And swiftly fade its flowers:
We've much to bear of grief and care,
But let us not forget –
The sun of hope and love will shine
Mid sorrow and regret.

There's something still worth living for,
If friendship hath not fled,
If love still in the bosom glows,
And feeling be not dead;
While these around our homes entwine
We've many a joy to bless –
And many a star to cheer us on
In darkness and distress.

There's something still worth living for
Though falsehood and deceit
In those whom we have truly loved,
Sometimes, perchance, we meet;
But let us nobly bear the worst
We fell of care and pain –
For after sorrow cometh joy
Like sunshine after rain.

Less than two years after writing this poem in 1864 Joseph Hutton was dead. Four of his 'fine healthy children' had already died one after the other of scarlet fever. Then his 'pet son' Edwin fell ill. Joseph Hutton himself became ill and died aged 44 in May 1866.

In the decade 1860–70 agitations for a reduction in working hours had achieved some success throughout the country, the Masons, Carpenters, and others having secured a 9-hour day. In 1871, after a four weeks' struggle, the Sunderland engineering employers conceded it. The movement clearly was not to be confined to Sunderland, and the master engineers of the North-Eastern district met at Newcastle to plan a united resistance to the demand, thus ensuring that any struggle in Newcastle, so far as one side could determine, would be a long one. It was. The strike lasted five months.

It was one of the notable events in trade union history, since the union organisation in the engineering trades of the Newcastle area was not strong at that time. A 'Nine Hours League' was formed, composed of unionists and non-unionists, and the struggle was conducted with skill by the leaders of this temporary organisation. When the strike had been in progress for some weeks financial support began to come from all quarters. It ended in victory for the League, and 54 hours was recognised as the working week in all the engineering trades.

This success excited the interest of the whole trade union movement, and it must have seemed to employers from one end of the country to the other that hours-reduction movements were as inevitable as spring showers or summer sunshine, or shall we say snow in winter! It would be a matter for surprised comment if it had not inspired the Bookbinders of London to new efforts.

The Manchester, Glasgow, Edinburgh and Dublin branches of the Consolidated Union has already scored some notable successes, and the London Branch, with the backing of the Central Committee, communicated with the London unions offering co-operation in a London movement. A joint Committee was formed, representing the London Consolidated Lodge, the Consolidated Union, and the Dayworking Bookbinders' Society.

This Committee decided to present to the London employers a memorial, which began:

> Gentlemen – the all-absorbing question of the day – *the diminution of the hours of labour and the social elevation of the working classes –* has doubtless afforded you food for serious consideration. The termination of the Newcastle-upon-Tyne dispute has led to extraordinary results. Open and determined resistance to this great social movement seems to have vanished altogether, and so rapid has been the change from antagonism to cohesion that it requires no great foresight to predict that at no very distant date nine hours will be a working day in this country.

Whether the Master Bookbinders were overwhelmed by the slightly florid Victorian phraseology of the memorial or demoralized by the rout of their engineering brethren in Newcastle or simply won by the justice of a request so reasonable must remain an open question, but the 9-hour day was secured with very little difficulty.

Thus, in the period between the strike by the early Bookbinder Lodges in 1786 and their imprisonment in 1787, and the efforts of the Consolidated Unions in the 'Short-Time Movement', generally called within the trade at the time the 'Nine-Hour Movement', 85 years after we find the hours of labour reduced from 75 to 54 hours per week and in the present day situation in 1983 down to 39 hours or less.

We sincerely hope that in our celebration year, and exhibition held at TUC on 28th June 1983, people did remember those who went and struggled before, and in many cases died, so we may reap the seeds of their labours.

·A·LITTLE·HOLIDAY: OR·A·DAY·OFF·FOR·ALL·PARTIES
[see "THE DONKEY & THE COMMON"]

Political Poster W. Crane.

THE DONKEY AND THE COMMON.

A FABLE.

A DONKEY once had the freedom of a delightful common. There was plenty of sweet grass to be had for the cropping, and though the fare varied with the course of the seasons, there was never a lack of thistles to give piquancy to the diet. Gorse bushes gave both perfume and shelter from the storms, and a cheap and easy roll could always be had in the sand pits, while common ponds served for drinking.

There were other donkeys who shared this rough and ready paradise, but as there was plenty of kicking room and no scarcity of pasture no serious differences arose, and I never heard of class distinctions being established between them and certain other commoners in the shape of geese, who were equally contented with the communal system. As our donkey was standing at ease one day, with pensive head and pendant ears of wisdom twitching with profound thought, there approached to him one of those beings called men whom he has been accustomed to despise on account of their only possessing two legs. This man, however, possessed, in addition to two legs, something of distinct interest to the donkey, namely, a bundle of hay. Friendly relations were soon established. There seemed no suspicion of overreaching commerce either in the transaction of handing over the hay—as in some cases where merchant venturers offer glass beads and hatchets for the native gold and ivory of simple tribes. The hay was simply handed by the one and eaten by the other. The two legs, however, began to move, supporting the bundle of hay at a convenient distance, and was followed unsuspectingly by the four legs, stimulated by an occasional mouthful. Thus the highway was reached, and then, without any warning, the two legs snatched the hay away, and, clapping a halter over the donkey's head, jumped upon his hind quarters, and, digging in its heels vigorously, with the accompaniment of a stick, forced the four legs to carry it along, with the bundle of hay.

The donkey resented: plunges and kickings and backings were the political measures resorted to, alternating with total abstention from movement.

Finally the legs were displaced from the seat of government and deposited by the wayside.

The donkey, free again, made his way back to the common; but other bipeds were busy putting a fence about it—they called it "enclosing"—and the donkey was beaten off. The owner of the hay coming up again took advantage of the situation, and a friend of his producing a bit and bridle, they were, under protest, fitted over the nose of the donkey. The two pairs of legs then mounted upon his back, and four legs, being for the time dumbfounded by these superior tactics, trotted humbly along, comforting themselves with prospective hay at the end of the journey.

Well, that journey's end did come at last; but it was in the murky streets of a squalid and smoky town, in a back yard and a tumble-down, draughty shed, with mouldy hay and water, and sore bones to boot. No springy turf, no gorse perfume, not even a thistle to bless oneself with. Thus mused the poor donkey, till heavy sleep, after the momentous fatigues of the day, overpowered him. He had not slept long, however, before his new masters roused him, and, hauling him out into the yard, put on the bridle, a heavy saddle, and two large pannikins to keep his balance true, filled with an abundance of tempting vegetables and fruit that he could not reach. The pair mounted again and rode him to the market place; but this only meant for the donkey the change of one load for another, without distinct improvement in his own fare, so that he was frequently in the position of one whose back is loaded with good things he cannot touch, glad to pick up garbage from the street to satisfy his hunger. "What a donkey I must have been to have left that common!" said he to himself.

This life of hard labour, rough usage, and scanty and poor fare went on for some time, and our donkey's fortunes showed but little sign of brightening.

Now and then he heard of donkeys revolting, but the only result seemed to be a tighter hand and heavier burdens.

One day, however (it was the first of May, too), came a change for him. His masters had driven him—for he was now promoted to the proud position of drawing a pair of wheels, which enabled his masters to make him draw much more weight than he formerly could carry upon his back—themselves included. Well, his masters had driven him to a common; that was something; but the common had a great cluster of tents and vans, with strange pictures on them. Wheels went round, with rows of wooden horses, to music; whistles blew and guns were shot off and there were crowds of people. It was very exciting altogether.

Our donkey was released from his cart, decked with ribbons, and his two masters, jumping on his back, drew him up in line with other donkeys with their riders.

It was a handicap donkey race. Off they started. It was a delight to feel the springy turf beneath the hoof again. The donkey needed no urging, for from animal spirits and old associations he went well. He went so well, indeed, and set the pace so fast that first one of his masters fell off, and then, after a futile struggle to keep his seat, and many blows, which only sent the donkey on faster, the other fell off, too, amid roars of laughter from the crowd of onlookers. The donkey, feeling his back free from any burden, won easily, and showed so much spirit and struck so stubbornly against returning to his life of toil that no one has ventured to ride or to coerce him since, and I have heard that he has got back to his common again and the enjoyment of his simple life.

Comment or moral is, perhaps, superfluous; but if one should read "natural man" or "worker" for "donkey," "land monopoly" for the first master, "capitalism" for the second, we can easily find details to fit "commercial competition," "the industrial system," and "the relation of labour to the employer," &c., in this homely fable.

WALTER CRANE.